D0021202

The
RED
EMBER
in the
WHITE
ASH

LLOYD JOHN OGILVIE

HARVEST HOUSE PUBLISHERS

EUGENE, OREGON

Unless otherwise indicated, all Scripture verses are taken from the New King James Version. Copyright ©1982 by Thomas Nelson, Inc. Used by permission. All rights reserved.

Verses marked NIV are taken from the HOLY BIBLE, NEW INTERNATIONAL VERSION®. NIV®. Copyright©1973, 1978, 1984 by the International Bible Society. Used by permission of Zondervan. All rights reserved.

Verses marked KJV are taken from the King James Version of the Bible.

Verses marked NASB are taken from the New American Standard Bible®, © 1960, 1962, 1963, 1968, 1971, 1972, 1973, 1975, 1977, 1995 by The Lockman Foundation. Used by permission. (www.Lockman.org)

Verses marked TLB are taken from The Living Bible, Copyright © 1971. Used by permission of Tyndale House Publishers, Inc., Wheaton, IL 60189 USA. All rights reserved.

Verses marked GNT are taken from the Good News Translation – Second Edition © 1992 by American Bible Society. Used by permission.

All emphasis in Scripture quotations has been added by the author.

Cover by Koechel Peterson & Associates, Inc., Minneapolis, Minnesota

Back-cover author photo © Mark Daniel Photography

THE RED EMBER IN THE WHITE ASH
Copyright © 2006 by Lloyd John Ogilvie
Published by Harvest House Publishers
Eugene, Oregon 97402
www.harvesthousepublishers.com

Library of Congress Cataloging-in-Publication Data

Ogilvie, Lloyd John.
 The red ember in the white ash / Lloyd John Ogilvie.
  p. cm.
 ISBN-13: 978-0-7369-1592-2 (hardcover)
 ISBN-10: 0-7369-1592-3
 Product # 6915923
 1. Resilience (Personality trait)—Religious aspects—Christianity. 2. Bible. N.T. Timothy, 2nd—Criticism, interpretation, etc. I. Title.
 BV4597.58.R47O47 2006
 248.4—dc22   2006006447

All rights reserved. No part of this publication may be reproduced, stored in a retrieval system, or transmitted in any form or by any means—electronic, mechanical, digital, photocopy, recording, or any other—except for brief quotations in printed reviews, without the prior permission of the publisher.

Printed in the United States of America

06 07 08 09 10 11 12 13 14 / RDS-KB / 10 9 8 7 6 5 4 3 2 1

To my wife, Doris—

who exemplifies enthusiasm for living
who epitomizes authentic resiliency
who exudes radiant joy

Acknowledgments

I'm very grateful to my friends Susie and Jason Salinas, who typed the manuscript of this book through several revisions. They are cherished friends whom I had the privilege to marry and whose son, Henry, I had the delight of baptizing. My wife, Doris, provided invaluable edits and insight to the manuscript. I'm also grateful to my assistant, Sandee Hastings, who gave administrative oversight to the process of completing my work on this book.

Contents

◼ ◼ ◼

Igniting a
Passion for Life

I think of writing a book as an honest, open, mutually stimulating dialogue with you, my reader. As in any good conversation between trusted friends, the topic usually gravitates to sharing what is on our minds.

Wherever I go these days, I find people who want to talk about a profound concern of their lives. These people fall into two categories: Those who have lost a passion for living, or those who fear they may lose it in the demands and distractions of life.

This book is about reigniting our passion for life. It's a conversation about what to do when our excitement, enthusiasm, and expectation for our future is like a red ember barely flickering in the white ash on the hearth of our heart. It is also about how the Lord can billow that red ember into a glowing flame that dances in our eyes, that brings radiance to our countenance, that glows in our personality, and that warms the shivering people in our life.

I've spent 50 years of my life working with people. This book has been written with you on my mind and your needs on my heart. I really care about what concerns you, and what I do know is that most everyone wants to live life to the fullest.

It is comforting to know that a key leader in the early church needed the red ember in the white ash of his heart billowed into flame again. His name was Timothy. He was a leader of the church at Ephesus. He was facing a kind of fear that made him cautious, reserved, and lacking in boldness and courage. What the apostle Paul wrote him from prison in Rome was like the apostle's last will and testament about the secrets of rejuvenation and resiliency. The secrets of recovering a passion for living that Paul shared with Timothy in AD 67 read like a survival kit for courageous living in confusing times.

Here, to my explanation of key verses in the book of 2 Timothy, which gives us the secret of authentic resiliency, I add the sharing of my own personal story, coupled with the accounts of the rejuvenation of real people who have recaptured a passion for living.

I pray that reading this book will be a conversation between us, and that your life, my valued reader and friend, will be more exciting than ever before.

Lloyd John Ogilvie

CHAPTER ONE

Billowing the Red Ember
in the White Ash

◥ ◣ ◥

All that was left in the hearth of the fireplace was white ash. The fire that had been blazing had burned down as the man shared with me what was happening in his life. He had asked me to come to his cabin in the woods at a conference center where I'd been speaking at a leadership seminar.

"I really need to talk with you," he had confided to me. I recognized him as a very successful leader of a company and a distinguished citizen of his community. And yet, his face revealed he was troubled. I had responded immediately to his invitation to come to his cabin for a confidential conversation. We sat in front of the fireplace, and he opened up about his diminishing excitement and enthusiasm for life.

The man's marriage of 30 years had lost its romance and excitement. Tender words of affection were seldom exchanged, and the closeness they had known had become strained. A sad sameness had settled in, and a boring blandness pervaded daily routines. His passion for life was at a low ebb.

The man was also troubled about his children. His main concern was that they didn't seem to share his convictions about life. He confessed he had not been able to pass on his faith. His two children had outward signs of success, but neither expressed the joy of knowing and serving God.

Another concern was for his decreasing enthusiasm for his job. He remembered the excitement he felt when he began his career. Going to work was a delight. However, as he had climbed up the ladder of leadership of his company and arrived at the top through hard work, his devotion to his job had been replaced by grim determination. Somehow, somewhere along the way, the fun had fizzled out.

I saw a bright red ember twinkling in the white ash!

I asked my new friend about his church. His response was disappointingly like so many religious people who need a fresh experience of spiritual resiliency. The church was not meeting his needs for revitalization. He was weary of lifeless traditions, dull preaching, and little help with living life with greater gusto and joy.

. . . .

Work on community boards and in social agencies had become a burden. My friend had been active in every cause imaginable. Now he felt drained and depleted.

Looking at the white ash in the hearth, suddenly he burst out, "Lloyd, that's just like my life! I was once ablaze like that fire was. Now look at what's left…nothing but burned-out ash."

I looked at the hearth again. To my surprise and delight, I saw a bright red ember twinkling in the white ash!

"Look at that red ember!" I exclaimed. "If we go out into the woods, gather some twigs and dry leaves for kindling, get a couple of logs from the stack next to the cabin, and then put a bellows to that red ember, this fireplace can glow again with a radiant fire."

A Parable in the Making

You guessed it. I sensed a living parable in the making that would provide me with a vivid response to what this man had told me about the diminished fires of passion for life in the hearth of his heart.

Like a couple of Boy Scouts, my new friend and I gathered the kindling and the logs. There was just enough life left in the red ember to billow it into a steady flame. We carefully placed the twigs and dry leaves over the new flame. Then I placed three logs over the burning kindling.

The number was very significant because of the example I was about to use as an illustration.

After expressing how I really empathized with what he was feeling, I shared with him the story of a first-century Christian leader of the church at Ephesus whose fires of passion needed to be stirred up and refueled. His name was Timothy.

It was in prison in Rome in the fall of AD 67 that the apostle Paul dictated his second letter to Timothy. While awaiting execution, the apostle had on his mind the future of the Christian movement. He particularly was concerned about Timothy, his son in the faith and the leader he had left in charge of the church in Ephesus, the Vanity Fair of the then-known world. Pagan worship in the Temple of Diana dominated the city with syncretism; the silversmiths controlled it with secularism. It was not an easy place to be a Christian or a leader of the church there.

Timothy had been converted to Christ when Paul had visited his hometown of Lystra on the first missionary journey. Young Timothy was encouraged in his spiritual growth by his grandmother Lois and his mother Eunice, both of whom had accepted Christ as Lord through the ministry of Paul. It was during his second missionary journey that Paul enlisted Timothy to be one of his missionary band as he moved around Galatia, Macedonia, Greece, and the province of Asia. Eventually Timothy was left in charge of the church at Ephesus.

Diminished Fires of Passion

Paul discerned the diminished fires of passion in Timothy. And yet, there was a red ember in the white ash in Timothy's hearth that needed to be stirred and billowed. "Therefore I remind you," Paul wrote Timothy, "to *stir up* the gift of God which is in you through the laying on of my hands" (2 Timothy 1:6). The apostle used a double-compound Greek word, *anazopurein,* in his admonition: *ana,* again; *zo,* life; *pur,* fire; thus, to stir—to billow into flame, rekindle, keep blazing.

The "gift" *(charisma)* of God was obviously the Holy Spirit; He is identified with spiritual fire in Scripture. John the Baptist predicted, "I…baptize you with water; but One mightier than I is coming…He will baptize you with the Holy Spirit and fire" (Luke 3:16). When Paul laid hands on Timothy and prayed for him, the young leader was set aflame with passion for Christ, love for people, and courage for leadership. Fellowship with Paul, Silas, and Luke kept the flame ablaze as they traveled together and stoked each other's fires.

Rekindling the Red Ember

A few years later Timothy was a lonely leader in Ephesus and needed a rekindling of the red ember within him. We are given a hint of the cause of the dampening of the flame in his heart by what Paul went on to write to him: "God has not given us a spirit of fear" (2 Timothy 1:7). The Greek word for fear here was not *phobos,* the word for fear most often used in the New Testament, but *deilias,* meaning caution, reserve, timidity, or cowardice. The word "spirit" in the phrase "a spirit of fear" means a pervading mood, attitude, or mode of thinking.

Deilias limits what we are willing to attempt to only those things we are sure we can pull off on our own strength, rather than by the Holy Spirit's power. The fires within our souls get smothered by negative thinking and quenched by feelings of inadequacy. Instead of being intrepidly bold, we become ineptly bound up in ourselves. We try to meet life's difficulties with our limited resources, and we neglect being refueled by the Spirit. The fires burn down because of life's demands. They never go out completely, however. There's always a red ember in the white ash waiting to be billowed into blaze again.

As I shared Timothy's story with my friend in front of the fireplace in his cabin, he identified with it immediately. In each of his relationships and responsibilities there had been a time when he had stopped trusting the Spirit's supernatural wisdom, discernment, vision, and creativity, and had taken over trying to press on depending on his human abilities alone. We talked at length about how the Lord always challenges us to trust Him when life's demands far exceed our human abilities.

Honestly, and openly, I confided my own experiences of consistently being pushed off plateaus of self-sufficiency to soul-stretching opportunities. In each case—in marriage, raising children, leading churches, or communicating hope through radio and television—I was constantly reminded of my inadequacy and the Lord's triumphant availability. Each time the fires burned low, I discovered I could ask for a fresh refueling of the fire of the Holy Spirit.

Where Has the Passion Gone?

Everywhere I go, I find people who are experiencing a diminished passion for life. The fires on the hearth of their hearts have slowly gone down. Life has a way of dampening the fires of excitement and enthusiasm for living. We burn down as our energies are sapped, our reserves are depleted, and our hopes smolder. People pressures get us down; problems pile up; worries and anxiety pour cold water on the previously blazing coals. As with my friend at the conference, things don't always work out as we've planned. Disappointment and discouragement stifle the flame of expectation about the future. Some people have intentionally kept the fire of the Spirit banked by neglect or resistance, or a dogged determination to limit what they think they can accomplish.

"Stir up the fires!" Paul urges. "God has not given us a spirit of fear." We can be sure of one thing: The spirit of fear does not come from God.

The Spirit of Fear

The spirit of fear is the direct opposite of genuine confidence. The concern, caution, and cowardice of the spirit of fear is what causes our lack of confidence in the stresses of life. It makes us fearful of failure, of losing people's approval, of feelings of inadequacy that straitjacket our creativity. Unfortunately, the deadly *fear* of inadequacy locks us into a real *level* of inadequacy.

Mark Twain had his tongue in his cheek when he said, "The human race is a race of cowards; and I'm not only marching in that procession, but carrying a banner." It's a lifelong challenge to stay out of that procession carrying a banner on which is written, "Keep safe at all costs!"

Robert Frost said, "There's nothing I'm afraid of like scared people." Sometimes we get scared realizing how easily we can get scared. We get fearful over our personal finances, losing the security of our jobs, and worry over our health.

Then too, the possibility of making mistakes sometimes causes us to be fearful. Charles Kettering said, "You never stub your toe standing still. The faster you go, the more chance there is of stubbing your toe, but the more chance you have of getting somewhere."

I like the great showman Eddie Cantor's advice to a young actor. It had more spiritual insight than he realized: "Why not get out on a limb? That's where the fruit is!" It's certainly where the fruit of the Spirit is. Love, joy, peace, patience, kindness, goodness, faithfulness, gentleness, and self-control are given by the Spirit in the pressures of life. Phillips Brooks knew this from his own experience: "You never become spiritual," he said, "by sitting down and wishing to become so. You must undertake something so great you cannot accomplish it unaided." But to attempt that, we need to get rid of the persistent nagging spirit of fear.

The Open Secret

Here's the secret: Our spirits were created to be filled with the fire of the Holy Spirit. He alone can burn up the chaff of fear that's the opposite of the confidence we need. It's not false self-confidence we need, but authentic Spirit-imputed confidence.

When we become Christians, the Holy Spirit assumes the responsibility for clearing up our thinking about the difference between true and false confidence. He takes some of us who are unduly confident in our limited talents and shows us what we could be as riverbeds for the flow of supernatural power. He helps us put our confidence in His absolutely resourceful reliability; as we accept bigger challenges than we ever thought we could accomplish, we learn He is faithful in helping us pull them off. We give Him the praise and begin to build up the confidence that Paul expressed: "I can do all things through Christ who strengthens me" (Philippians 4:13).

For some of us, the spirit of fear is caused by debilitatingly low self-esteem. We need a healed self-image, a picture of what we would be like filled with the enthusiasm and expectation of the fire of the Spirit. We need a release from memories of past mistakes that produce a fear of future failure. In our relationships the spirit of fear often is manifested in worry over rejection and being hurt. The Holy Spirit seeks to convince us of how much we are cherished. He reminds us of the Father's care and Christ's cross. Then he builds up our sense of being valued, and in each circumstance, He engenders clarity about what we should attempt and what we can accomplish.

Fuel for the Fire

But it's one thing to know what we are to do; it's quite another to attempt it. After telling Timothy that "God has not given us a spirit of fear" the apostle Paul goes on to explain what He has given us. He follows up by offering us "power, love, and a sound mind." My friend was eager to hear about that. We talked at length about the power of the Holy Spirit.

Jesus had promised power to live life to the fullest. "You shall receive power when the Holy Spirit has come upon you," He assured His disciples. It happened at Pentecost. Since then the power fuel for passionate living has been the indwelling Spirit. He gives us power to do what Christ calls us to do: to love, forgive, share our faith, endure the pressure of daily life, and battle for justice in every realm of life. He brings to our memory Christ's message and helps us to live it. He works in us to energize us to envision what He will enable us to do: "…to Him who is able to do exceedingly abundantly above all that we ask or think, *according to the power that works in us,* to Him be glory in the church by Christ Jesus to all generations, forever and ever" (Ephesians 3:20-21).

The power that works in us is the Holy Spirit, moving within us in perfect harmony with the Father and the reigning Christ. The Greek word for power used by Paul in his bracing admonition to Timothy was *dunameos,* meaning instigating, implementing, initiative strength.

Whenever the fire burns down on the hearth of my heart, I reread one of James Stewart's salient statements. Dr. Stewart was my professor of New Testament Studies at New College, Edinburgh, Scotland. What I heard him thunder forth in class was later published in a sermon:

. . . .

It is God's way to go beyond the best that He has done before; therefore a living faith will always have in it a certain element of surprise and tension and discovery; that what we have seen and learned of God up to the present is not to be the end of our seeing nor the sum total of our learning; that whatever we have found in Christ is only a fraction of what we still can find; that the spiritual force which in the great days of the past vitalized the church and shaped the course of history has not exhausted its energies or fallen into abeyance but is liable at any moment to burst out anew and take control. God is promising wonders that he has never done before so that there will be more jubilant doxologies, more exultant hallelujahs. For there is no limit to the creative love of God, no end to the redeeming grace of Christ, *and no exhaustion of the power of the Holy Spirit.*[1]

This assurance of the inexhaustible power of the Holy Spirit has been the compelling conviction of my life. Whenever I have sensed the need for fresh fuel on the flame in my heart, He has replenished me with power I could never have produced on my own.

I shared this realization with my friend there in the cabin before the fireplace. As I did I put a log on the now flaming kindling. "That's the power of the Holy Spirit. Placing that

log on the hearth of our hearts is a crucial first step in stirring up the fire. An honest prayer does it. Simply say, 'Holy
Spirit, I need Your power; I ask for Your power; I want to be
set ablaze with your power.'"

Love Is the Purpose

The power of the Holy Spirit is for a purpose. It is closely related to the second aspect of the antidote to a spirit of
fear that Paul shared with Timothy: "God has not given us a
spirit of fear, but of power *and of love.*" We have discussed
how true power replaces the spirit of *deilias*—caution, timidity, reserve, even cowardice. Now we are ready to allow the
Holy Spirit to make us people who are glowing with radiant love—a very different quality of love than what mas-
querades as love in our culture. I want to explain this debilitating, destructive law that governs this distorted love so
we can resist being part of practicing it.

The False Law of Relationships

The relational law of our culture goes something like
this: He who loves least holds most power. The person who
withdraws or withholds love often holds the power position in a relationship. Allow me to illustrate as follows.

It happens in marriage. One of the two persons can
gain unfair control by withdrawing love through withholding words, actions, and expressions of love. When

either a husband or wife shuts down on the other, the tendency of the mate is to wonder what he or she did. *What's wrong? What did I do? What can I say or be to make things right again?* The person who is holding out soon discovers he or she also holds great control. The problem is this can become a bad habit used too frequently until the marriage drifts onto the rocks. Stingy lovers make strained marriages.

The same is true for our relationships in the family. Parents often try to control children's behavior with withdrawn love. A quid pro quo is used to keep children in line. Acceptance, affirmation, praise, and delight are withheld in a vain expectation of gaining or keeping control. No wonder some young adults find it difficult to accept the unqualified love of a heavenly Father, or the unlimited grace of an accepting Savior, or the unrestrained encouragement of an always available Holy Spirit.

But children can also try to control their parents by refusing to express the love every parent longs to receive. Some children rule the roost by ungrateful behavior and unexpressed affection. Amazing how many parents try to win the approval of their children, especially in the teen or young adult years. Equally amazing is how many children learn how to manipulate the parents with bartered love.

The law of love in our culture is also expressed in friendship. Again, the withdrawal of love gets the other person's attention. It can be a shout or a pout, but it helps us get the control we falsely desire. Criticism, judgmentalism, aloof displeasure, or just plain neglect awakens a friend to the disturbing realization something is wrong. "What happened?" we ask. The friend has gained the leverage.

The church is not exempt. Often culture invades the church, and this same distorted relational law—he who loves least holds most power—is expressed in the relationship of clergy and church members. Giving or withholding approval or approbation is a powerful force. Church members sometimes seek to control clergy by lack of support, stingy encouragement, or critical attitudes. Some clergy adjust their leadership, the level of passion with which they preach, or their confrontation of critical social issues to please their constituents and keep a steady flow of giving. Equally true is that some clergy lack warm encouraging love for their people. In some cases, a pastor's attitude and demeanor communicate a lack of contagious delight in his or her people. Sometimes preaching that's passed off as prophetic has a lot of anger expressed in it. As one teenager asked his dad, "Why was the pastor so mad at us this morning?" The sermon was on grace!

Too often culture's law of distorted love is practiced in the marketplace. The question is, how does a manager get and keep the loyalty, respect, industry, and productivity of the people who report to him or her? The positive way is to define clear goals, provide good working conditions, express affirmation and encouragement, and expect responsible productivity and accountability. Often just the opposite is the norm. Employers try to control employees through the threat of losing their jobs, being bypassed for advancement, lack of raises, or withheld praise and recognition. On the other hand, employees can seek to gain control by lack of cooperation and a commitment to excellence.

Countercultural Christians

We are called to be countercultural Christians and go against the false law of relationships. It is the Holy Spirit's assignment to help us live what I like to call the eleventh commandment. Christ said,

> A new commandment I give to you, that you love one another; as I have loved you, that you also love one another. By this all will know that you are My disciples, if you have love for one another (John 13:34-35).

We are called to be supernaturally empowered people who express love that is indefatigable, honest, remedial, and healing. The flame of the Holy Spirit enables us to radiate the love Jesus defined. The Spirit engenders faith to believe in Christ as Lord and Savior, empowers us with hope for the people in our lives, and actually imbues us with an aptitude to love far beyond our human ability.

Love Is Primary

The Holy Spirit is love. Remember that love is the primary fruit of the Spirit. He is the love that is required to live out Jesus' new commandment to love as He has loved us. Most of us would admit that the Holy Spirit has a big assignment with people like us. Sometimes His flame flickers in us, and we need to be refueled to overcome our tendency

> *I shared with my friend how we can become radiant, initiative lovers of people.*

to make condemnatory judgments and write off people who have hurt us, to focus on the troubling memories of what they have said and done. Often we tire of serving others by loving the way Jesus loved. Then it is time to stir up the fire. When we ask the Holy Spirit to renew the flame of love, He does help us to love when we'd rather reject people ruthlessly, judge mercilessly, or condemn angrily. Most of all He reminds us that we are loved unqualifiedly, and He gives us the strength to love people unstintingly. Put that log on the fire and feel the warmth increase.

I did just that as I shared with my friend how we can become radiant, initiative lovers of people. He tried that on as he considered how much he needed supernatural love flaming in his life.

A Sound Mind

We were not finished. There was a third log to be added to the fire. "God has not given us a spirit of fear, but of power and of love and of *a sound mind*." The fire of the Spirit is also a refining fire that produces a healed mind capable of self-control.

The Greek word for "sound mind" is a double compound noun, *sōphronismou*. Taken literally, it is a combination of *so* from *sozo*—meaning "heal, whole"—and *phron* from *phronema*, the attitudinal mind (as used in *phroneite* in Philippians 2:5: "Have in you this *mind* which was in Christ Jesus"). It is derived from a late *koinē* Greek word, *sophronizō*, to control. So the stirring up of the gift of God with *sōphronismou* is to have our attitudinal mind healed so we can trust the Lord for what He alone can control—and take control of what He has placed in our control.

We can't do that without the healing of two crucial aspects of our thinking brain: memory and imagination.

Healing of Memories

The healing of memories is a strategic step in the refining ministry of the Holy Spirit. The fire of authentic passion for living, loving people, and making a difference where we work and in the community where we reside cannot burn when quenched by haunting memories. Stirring up the fire requires time alone with the Holy Spirit as our counselor. When we ask Him, He will help us excavate disturbing memories that make us fearful. Our part is to pray for the exposure of anything in the past that immobilizes us, keeping us from being bold, courageous, shining lights in a dark world. Jesus calls us to let our lights shine. We can't do that when we are obsessed with our past failures and other people's actions or words.

Find time to be quiet in fellowship with the Holy Spirit. Pray, "Holy Spirit, I trust You as the Counselor Christ promised. Expose anything that keeps my fires banked. Heal my troubling memories."

Liberation of Imagination

The Holy Spirit also liberates our imagination to ignite a new excitement for the future. We all are in the process of becoming the person we imagine in our mind's eye. We have been endowed with the capacity to envision the future, to picture what we are meant to do and be in life's relationships and responsibilities. The Holy Spirit's further assignment is to help us discern God's will.

The Spirit is the source of vision. We can trust Him. He can set our wills on fire with a glowing determination to act on the guidance He reveals. We can claim 1 Corinthians 2:9-12:

Eye has not seen, nor ear heard, nor have entered into the heart of man the things which God has prepared for those who love Him. But God has revealed them to us through His Spirit. For the Spirit searches all things, yes, the deep things of God. For what man knows the things of a man except the spirit of the man which is in him. Even so no one knows the things of God except the Spirit of God. Now we have received not the spirit of the world, but the Spirit who is from God, that we might know the things that have been freely given to us by God.

Then in the sixteenth verse, Paul states the momentous truth: "Who has known the mind of the LORD that he may instruct Him? But we have the mind of Christ." Through the Spirit we are able to discern not only what Christ would do, but also what He would have us do with the people in our lives and the circumstances we must face.

Creative Self-Control

The result of the healing of debilitating memories and the release of creative imagination is the ability to control the unique self each of us is. For me, this has meant burning intentionality, putting into action the best intentions instigated in me by the Holy Spirit. Self-control is not the opposite of turning the control of our lives over to the Lord;

rather it is the implementation of what we discover we are to do under His control. We take control by being willing to do the Lord's will. The more we obey the orders given us, the more clarity we will have about specific action steps. I've found that the Spirit answers our prayers for guidance with yes, no, or later. He also provides intellectual clarity, emotional assurance, and volitional determination.

One of the best examples of how the Spirit produces authentic self-control is Connie Mack. With his permission, I've often told his story in my writing and speaking. While he was a senator from Florida, he faithfully attended the Thursday noon senators' Bible study I taught as Chaplain of the Senate.

One Thursday, I felt led to ask if anyone present wanted to receive fresh power from the Holy Spirit. A long five minutes of silence ensued. Connie at first resisted the invitation, then suddenly found himself raising his arm and saying, "I'm ready, Chaplain. I want you to pray for me." He recalls having no idea what this would mean or what he would experience subsequently.

The other senators gathered around him, and I simply asked these questions: "Connie, are you ready to commit your life to Christ? Are you ready to commit your ministry as a United States Senator to be a servant-leader? Are you willing to receive the Holy Spirit's supernatural gifts of knowledge, discernment, vision, and prophetic power, to boldly declare the truth as it is revealed to you?" Connie responded with a resounding "Yes!" to each of these questions. When he stood up, his face was radiant.

Senator Mack's reflections on that day and a subsequent experience tell in a very pointed way how the Holy Spirit stirs up the fire in our souls:

"There is no adequate way to express the emotions of that moment, but as I looked back on it a few weeks later, I understood what was happening. I had a sense of something gushing out of me—my control of my life—and the beginning of turning over control of my life to God. I stress the word *beginning* because of what happened later.

"My wife, Priscilla, and I were in Vermont. It was cold and snowing. I enjoyed an afternoon of quiet reading—a book about the Holy Spirit as the greatest Counselor in the world. Later in the afternoon, I decided to go snowshoeing through the woods. Deep in the woods, I had an experience I'll never forget. It was so quiet. The only sounds were the branches of trees rubbing against each other.

"The gentle breeze was like the movement of the Holy Spirit. At that moment, I had this sense of prayer. I actually wanted to get down on my knees, but being a Florida boy, and having snowshoes strapped on my feet, I wasn't sure if I got on my knees I could get back up. So, I stood there and lifted my hands to the heavens and prayed that God would fill me with His Holy Spirit. There was a sense of the infilling of the Spirit—love, joy, peace, patience, goodness, kindness, gentleness, faithfulness, self-control—and the feeling that I would be able to share these qualities with people I meet."

And now, some years later, Connie Mack continues to radiate the glow of the indwelling Holy Spirit.

When I shared Connie's experience with the man at the leadership conference, he expressed a desire to have me pray for him as I had for Connie. So there in front of the now-blazing fire—rebuilt with the three logs I've described as symbols of the power, love, and sound mind the Holy Spirit offers us as an antidote to the spirit of timidity, caution, and cowardice—I prayed for him. I'm happy to report it was the turning point for the man. For the first time in his life, he asked to be ignited by the fire of the Holy Spirit. I've kept in touch with him since that night, and each time we talk I sense the excitement, enthusiasm, and expectancy of being an on-fire Christian.

Billows of Blessing

As you read this, the Holy Spirit is ready to put a bellows to the red ember in the white ash of the hearth of your heart. He stirs up the red ember, blows off the white ash, and then, to replace the spirit of fear, fuels the flickering flame with power, love, and a sound mind.

You and I were meant to be on fire!

. . . .

What I've tried to communicate in this chapter is expressed in a poem by my friend Sue McCollum, which she wrote after hearing my message about the red ember in the white ash.

> *Within my heart is a red ember*
> *   where once a fire used to be.*
> *A small red ember amidst the white ash*
> *   is all that's inside of me.*
>
> *My heart used to be a mighty blaze,*
> *   I had great passion for the Lord.*
> *I thought I could conquer mountains,*
> *   but now I sit here bored.*
>
> *The blaze became a little flame,*
> *   and then a small red ember.*
> *Lost I was in the white ash,*
> *   my God I could hardly remember.*
>
> *But God did not let me go*
> *   but on that ember He blew.*
> *He set my heart aflame again*
> *   and created me anew.*[2]

CHAPTER TWO

Opening the Damper— The Dynamics of a Twofold Commitment

E very fire on a hearth needs a good draft of air flowing beneath it and through it up into the flue. We must open the damper to allow the draft to be drawn through. The same is true for the fire on the hearth of our hearts. Over the years I've discovered there is a dual commitment required to open the damper in our lives and allow the wind of the Spirit to move over and through the embers He has ignited in us. What is this dual commitment? Allow me to explain.

Starting in verse 9 of the first chapter of his second letter to Timothy, Paul goes on to remind the young leader of who he is, to Whom he belongs, and for what he was destined. Astounding assurances are communicated. He was singled out to receive grace and a holy calling before time began, he had experienced new life in Christ, and he had been entrusted with the gospel, the good news of Christ's life, cross, resurrection, and reigning power. The Lord had a purpose and plan for Timothy.

A Call to Commitment

To respond, Timothy needed to make a commitment like Paul's. "I know whom I have believed and am persuaded that He is able to keep what I have committed to Him until that Day" (1:12). Paul's commitment was in direct response to a renewed realization of what he had been called to be and do.

Then the apostle turns to Timothy and sounds the clarion call for his response of commitment. But there's a difference. Note carefully that Paul says, "That good thing which was committed to you, keep by the Holy Spirit who dwells in us" (1:14). Timothy was to learn from the apostle the true meaning of an unreserved commitment, and in turn his commitment was to keep what was committed to him. There are two aspects to a dual commitment: what is committed to us, and what we commit to the Lord.

The Greek word translated as "committed," *paratheken,* literally means a deposit committed to another person's trust for safekeeping. In Paul's time there were no banks, so there was no more trusted duty than to accept the responsibility of another person's valuables. An equally high trust was to allow a person to invest your money for you and then return to you the interest earned. The Greek word for "keep," *phulaxai,* means to guard against robbery or loss. It also implies investment at high return.

The words "committed" and "keep" are linked closely together. Paul has committed his total life unreservedly to Christ. It is as if he were saying, "There's no doubt in my mind about Christ's reliability. I know him personally and have learned that He is able, has all power, to multiply my effectiveness in whatever I completely turn over to His control." Then to Timothy he says, in essence, "Multiply what the Lord has entrusted to you with unreserved willingness."

Dynamic Dual Commitment

This is how the dual commitment works. When we commit our lives and all our needs and concerns on a daily basis to the Lord, He does entrust them back to us to do what He wills with His constant guidance and power. Specific things that are committed for us to do and be become clear. Then we commit ourselves to obedient follow-through. In response, the Lord commits to us His faithfulness, guidance, and the power of the Holy Spirit. We are never left to struggle through on our own. The Father watches over us, Christ goes before us to show the way, and the Holy

Spirit sets us on fire with the excitement, enthusiasm, and expectancy we've been talking about. But we must open the damper. That's our part. It's an act of will to commit to do what the Lord has committed to us. Dual commitment begins when we make our initial commitment, but it must be repeated daily, hourly, in the challenges and opportunities committed to us by the Lord.

My Own Experience

Allow me to be personal about this. My first commitment was made when I was 18. I was a freshman at Lake Forest College in Lake Forest, Illinois. At a Bible study in my dormitory, I heard about the exciting adventure of knowing and following Jesus Christ as my Lord and Savior. I was challenged to turn over the control of my life to Christ and become His disciple. Every part of my being was involved. I was intellectually convinced that Christ had died for me, had forgiven me, and was calling me to serve Him. Emotionally, I responded to Christ's unqualified grace for me. I felt loved, accepted, and affirmed. Volitionally, I willed to surrender the

The traumatic transition from willful self-control to the Lord's control consists of relinquishment, reassurance, and rejuvenation.

management of my life to Christ. That night in 1948, the fire of the Holy Spirit began to burn within me.

However, that was only the beginning. A character transplant began, my faith began to grow, my mind was expanded with dynamic biblical truth, and my soul was stretched by challenges way beyond my human abilities. There was a fire burning within me, but the secret for keeping that fire growing and blazing was one I discovered early in my Christian life and have relearned again and again. That secret is the thrust of this chapter.

Simply put, and once more for emphasis, dual commitment must be expressed constantly, day by day, as the years roll by. The Lord presses us on with new problems to solve, new potential to grasp, and new power to receive. He commits to us what we in turn must commit back to Him. The traumatic transition from willful self-control to the Lord's control consists of relinquishment, reassurance, and rejuvenation. All three are part of opening the damper and receiving the draft that fans the fires within us.

Relinquishment

Relinquishment is the key to becoming an on-fire Christian. Many people who believe in Christ have never relinquished the management of their lives to Him. Over my years of pastoral ministry and the Chaplaincy in the U.S. Senate, some of the most moving moments have been when church members and traditional Christians who did not know Christ personally have responded to the challenge to commit their lives to Him. I've seen it happen to church members, church officers, clergy, and senators. The damper is opened, and the draft blows on the red embers. People realize the wonderful gift of life the Lord has committed to them. They respond by the relinquishment of their total life to Him.

But that's only the beginning. Committed Christians receive a holy calling. They realize the Lord had them in mind before time began—and He has something He wants to do through them that will not be done unless they make a commitment to do it and follow through.

In the Bible studies I was privileged to lead in the Senate with senators, spouses of senators, and staff, we developed a motto made up of eight words: "Without God we can't; without us, He won't." We can't do anything without the Lord's power, but He waits for our commitment to release that power. All of us are in the place we are by God's plan and purpose. We have a realm made up of our relationships and responsibilities.

When I ask people if they have ever made a commitment of their lives, I'm amazed at how many say they have never relinquished their wills to the Lord. When I listen to people tell me about their problems, I'm equally amazed at how many have never made a specific relinquishment of their need by making a complete commitment of it to the Lord.

Reassurance

When we do relinquish ourselves, the Lord gives us the reassurance He is committed to help us. He has invested a great deal in us; He is counting on us to do His will in our realm. He is faithful. Jesus exemplified the power of relinquishment and reassurance on the first day of the last week of His incarnate life and ministry. As recorded in John 12, after the triumphal entry into Jerusalem, some Greeks came to Jesus' disciple Philip, saying, "Sir, we wish to see Jesus." Philip got Andrew, and the two of them told Jesus. It was a sign that the hour of the cross was drawing near. Jesus taught about the cross, "Most assuredly, I say to you, unless a grain of wheat falls into the ground and dies, it remains alone; but if it dies, it produces much grain" (verse 24). Then Jesus declared the paradox: When we love our lives, we will lose them; but if we lose our lives, we will find them. It is in dying to self that we live.

Then at the height of the intensity of His teaching, He cried out to God the four words that are the essence of commitment: "Father, glorify Your name" (verse 28). The prayer of relinquishment is for God to manifest His character in the problem, perplexity, or potential we are facing. The name of God is synonymous with the character of God. He glorifies His name when He balances our need with an intervention of an aspect of His character to outweigh what we are facing. He enters into our complexity with His goodness, faithfulness, grace, and strength.

What the Father said in response to Jesus' prayer of relinquishment that day is exactly the reassurance He communicates to us: "I have both glorified it [My name] and will glorify it again" (verse 28). To know that God knows—and will act to help us in time and on time—is the source of peace in the trouble, serenity in the storm, and strength in the stress. Reassurance grows as we remember salient "He is able" passages, such as "He is able to aid those who are tempted" (Hebrews 2:18); "He is also able to save to the uttermost" (7:25): He "is able to keep you from stumbling" (Jude 24); He "is able to establish you" (Romans 16:25). Especially germane to our consideration of commitment is what we quoted earlier, "He is able to keep what I have committed to Him" (2 Timothy 1:12).

Reassurance grows in us as we let go of our concerns or challenges. In what areas of your life are you clenching your fists and saying, "I've got to take care of this myself"? Open those fists and put the needs into the trustworthy hands of our Lord. He's worthy of the trust. He's been handling people and their problems since the creation of humankind. Open the draft!

Rejuvenation

When we open the draft, rejuvenation results. With the fire on the hearth, the oxygen in the flow of air replenishes the fire. The actual meaning of rejuvenation is a transformation that imparts renewed vitality. It also means to reinvigorate what has burned down so that it suddenly bursts back to its original strength and glow. Spiritually, it means reclaiming hope and expectation again.

Returning to the account of Jesus' conversation with the Father in John 12, notice that after the Father's answer, "I have both glorified it and will glorify it again," Jesus was able to express amazing rejuvenation. He could look into the foreboding days ahead and see that God would bring ultimate good out of the worst that could be imagined: "I, if I am lifted up from the earth, will draw all people to Myself" (verse 32). God would glorify His name at Calvary. During those six hours of the once-done, never-to-be-repeated, cosmic atonement for the sins of the world and the reconciliation of humankind to Himself, God manifested His name in judgment and justification.

During His ministry on earth, Jesus made it very clear that to follow Him we must take up our cross. Commitment involves a diminutive cross for all of us. Surrender of our lives means death to our willful self and resurrection of a new self, a new creation.

An Everyday Cross

Some time ago, I was in a jewelry store. A woman came in and asked the clerk where the store displayed its crosses. She was led to a glass counter in which a magnificent display of cosmetic crosses was artfully arranged. After she surveyed the jeweled crosses, she said, "Oh no, I just want an everyday kind of cross." As she continued shopping by looking over the plain gold or silver crosses, I mulled over the phrase, *just an everyday cross.*

The adjective "everyday" is descriptive of the cross of commitment we experience repeatedly through the days of our discipleship. The cross was then on Calvary, but it is also now as we live through the recapitulation of the death and resurrection cycle in daily relinquishment and new rejuvenation. Paul wrote the Galatians,

> I have been crucified with Christ; it is no longer
> I who live, but Christ lives in me; and the life
> which I live in the flesh I live by faith in the Son
> of God who loved me and gave Himself for me
> (Galatians 2:20).

The apostle also spoke of dying daily to self.

The Greek word for daily in Christ's call to take up our cross daily is *hēmeran,* a daily act. However, the adjective for daily in the petition "Give us this day our daily bread" in the Lord's Prayer is distinctly different. It is *epiousion,* a combination of *epi* ("upon") and *eimi* ("to be"). We are to pray for bread for what is to be—bread for going on, or bread for the morrow. "Give us today the bread we need for tomorrow."

In the context of what we are discovering about an everyday cross as the essence of true commitment on a daily basis, today's commitment provides us supernatural strength for tomorrow. Today's personal Calvary, death to self, makes way for resurrection living tomorrow. The cross of Christ and our daily cross are two inseparable, inescapable aspects of commitment. We can't bypass the cross.

There's a contemporary song that reminds me I can't slip around Golgotha's cross or my daily cross.

> It's not conservative or liberal
> However they're defined;
> It's not about interpretation,
> Or the judgment of the mind;
>
> It's the opposite of politics,
> Power or prestige;
> It's about a simple message,
> And whether we believe.
>
> We can water down theology
> And preach a word to suit our needs;
> We can justify sweet subtle lies,
> That are wrapped in noble deeds;

We can alter our convictions,
To adapt to social whims;
But we cannot change the gospel
Or the truth contained within.

It's still the cross,
It's still the blood of Calvary
That cleanses sins
And sets the captives free.

It's still the name,
The name of Jesus
That has power to save the lost;
It's still the cross.[3]

And I would add: It's still the cross that's the heart of the dual commitment that brings daily contentment.

Now, let's be very specific about the dual commitment in your life and mine.

1. Have I ever made an unreserved commitment to Christ in addition to believing in Him as Lord and Savior?

2. Am I living out the threefold dynamic of relinquishment, reassurance, and rejuvenation on a daily basis?

3. What has the Lord committed to me that now must be committed back to Him so I can accomplish it by His strategy and strength?

. . . .

4. Am I more on fire today with conviction and courage as the result of daily commitment than I was yesterday?

Don't Dampen the Fire

Paul admonished the Thessalonians, "Do not quench the Spirit" (1 Thessalonians 5:19). The word "quench" in the Greek means *to dampen*. How do you put out a fire? You can douse it with water, or you can close the damper and deprive it of a draft. We all know what happens when the damper is closed. A smoldering fire sputters and flickers and eventually goes out. If you don't feed a fire, it won't grow. It loses its glow. The opposite of quenching is to fuel the fire in our heart's hearth by daily, hour-by-hour commitment of what we have discerned the Lord has committed to us to be and do.

Consistent commitment makes all of life exciting. It means turning over every circumstance and relationship, each new difficulty or decision, to Him—and then giving thanks in the midst of everything because of the release from the stress and tension of our own control. Quenching the Holy Spirit is refusing to allow the flame of His presence to glow brightly, but we are meant to be radiant and alive with love. Our eyes are meant to dance with joy. There should be such a warmth from our countenance that others are drawn magnetically not just to us, but to the Lord to whom we have made our initial and daily commitment.

One of my favorite quotes about commitment is based on some thoughts of Goethe. I keep it on my desk and often place it on a podium when I speak. I've gone back to it, both in the valley of trouble, and on the plateaus of success when I need to press on in the adventure of discipleship. Reading it and living it opens the damper for the flow of the draft beneath and through the fire on the hearth of our hearts.

> The moment one definitely commits oneself, then Providence moves too. All sorts of things occur to help one that would never otherwise have occurred. A whole stream of events issues from the decision, raising in one's favor all manner of unforeseen incidents and meetings and material assistance, which no one could have dreamed would come his way. "Whatever you can do, or dream you can do, begin it. Boldness has genius, power, and magic in it."
>
> Begin it now.[4]

CHAPTER THREE

Stoking with Strength

W hen I was a boy in Kenosha, Wisconsin, the winter mornings were bitter cold. Frost would cover the windows and the blustery winds would beat against my family's house.

I can remember poking my head out from under the covers and seeing my breath in the chilly air in my bedroom. I would snuggle down under the covers waiting as long as I could before I had to get up for breakfast and the trudge through the snow to school.

It was an assurance of my dad's care for the family when I would hear him get up before the rest of us and go down into the basement to stoke the furnace by poking the coals that had almost burned out during the night. Then I would hear his big shovel scrape along the floor of the coal bin and then scoop up coal that he would shovel into the furnace. When the fire was ablaze, the warm air would rise through the ducts and into the radiator in my room.

◪ ◪ ◪

I think of this childhood experience whenever I reflect on stoking the fires of the Spirit within me. To stoke a physical fire means to supply a furnace with fuel. Again, the metaphor has an impact on our thinking about the fire in the hearth of our hearts.

Sometimes before I get up in the morning, I pull up the covers and think and pray about the day ahead. Most every day has its own share of tasks, challenges, problems, and burdens, as well as splendid opportunities, exciting possibilities, and awesome blessings in the making. Before I put my foot on the floor and start the day I'm very aware of how much I need supernatural strength for the day ahead. There's a great difference between saying, "Good Lord, what a morning!" and "Good morning, Lord."

Some days we'd all like to stay in bed and avoid the pressures and stress of the day ahead. That's just not possible. That kind of denial soon would lead to depression, and eventually, defeat.

But, have you ever stayed in bed long enough to review the day ahead and realized how much you need strength?

Often in the morning before I get up, I repeat some lines from a poem by Annie Johnston Flint:

> *God hath not promised*
> *Skies always blue,*
> *Flower-strewn pathways*
> *All our lives through;*
> *God hath not promised*
> *Sun without rain,*
> *Joy without sorrow,*
> *Peace without pain.*
>
> *But God hath promised*
> *Strength for the day,*
> *Rest for the labor,*
> *Light for the way,*
> *Grace for the trials,*
> *Help from above,*
> *Unfailing sympathy,*
> *Undying love.*[5]

Strength for the day? The stoking of the fires of the Spirit within us adds fuel to provide us with the strength we will need.

The Strength of Christ's Grace

What exactly, though, is the strength we need most, and how do we receive it? The word in the Greek of the New

Testament usually used for "strength" is the word for power, *dunamis*. It's used in various forms, but the essential meaning is the same: intellectual power through the inspiration of the Spirit; emotional power to receive and communicate love, joy, peace, kindness, endurance, and faithfulness enabled by the Spirit; volitional strength to will, to act on the Spirit's guidance; physical strength beyond our normal level of energy.

Paul wanted Timothy to receive a particular quality of strength. Actually, it is the strength that makes possible all other kinds of strength. Verse 1 of chapter 2 of 2 Timothy is a bracing challenge to be strong, as well as a reminder of the source of that strength. Frequently, throughout this epistle to Timothy, the apostle introduces exhortations with the Greek expression *su oun* or *su de*, meaning "you therefore" or "but you." The implication is, "as for you." This expression is used to emphasize what is expected of Timothy regardless of what is happening around him or the mood or actions of others around him.

> *"Don't worry about what others are thinking or doing...be strengthened in the grace that is in Christ Jesus."*

The verse, "You therefore, my son, be strong in the grace that is in Christ Jesus" (2:1) might be transliterated or paraphrased as follows: "Don't worry about what others are thinking or doing, and don't focus on how weak and inadequate you may feel. As for you, Timothy, be strengthened in the grace that is in Christ Jesus."

The verb, "be strong," as it is used in this verse, *endunamon*, is in the passive. The strength is not something Timothy was to produce himself. It was a gift he was to receive. When so many around him were showing weakness, Timothy's challenge was to allow the fires within him to be stoked by the strength of the grace that was offered him in Christ Jesus.

I'm convinced that Paul's admonition to Timothy came from the apostle's own experience of receiving the strength of Christ's grace. In 2 Corinthians 12:7-10, Paul shares his struggle with a physical malady he called a "thorn in the flesh." When he had prayed three times for it to be removed, Christ had said, "My grace is sufficient for you, for My strength is made perfect in weakness" (verse 9). The Greek word *arkie* from *arkeō* translated as "sufficient," means "enough" or "what we need." Christ's strength, *dunamis*, accomplishes its purpose in our weakness. Paul's realization of this secret of receiving strength enabled him to exclaim,

> Therefore, most gladly I will rather boast in my infirmities, that the power of Christ may rest upon

me. Therefore, I take pleasure in infirmities, in reproaches, in needs, in persecutions, in distresses, for *Christ's sake*. For when I am weak, then I am strong (verse 10).

What does this mean for you and me? We can be made strong by receiving strength at our weakest point.

This is true for our whole life and for each day. Our point of weakness that initially brings us to Christ becomes the corridor of need down which He comes to us. It may be a conviction of our sin, or of a character proclivity, that shows us how much we need to change. Or, it may be a behavioral problem that constantly debilitates our relationships—selfishness, pride, manipulative control issues, an unforgiving spirit, a condemnatory judgmentalism, an insecurity that keeps us a small package all wrapped up in ourselves. Christ comes to us with transforming power. He makes us new people by his grace, and then reforms our character to emulate His own.

The secret of strength, that we can be made strong at our weakest point, is also true for our daily living. Where are you feeling weak today? Where do you need an infusion of strength? Where do I? When we identify our particular weakness each day, that becomes the area of a deeper relationship with the Lord. Our weakness is made perfect, that is, accomplishes its purpose, by opening us up to a new stoking with strength.

The way we are strengthened is *in* the grace that is *in* Christ Jesus. Don't miss the infinitives, those little words, "in." To be in Christ Jesus is to be in a profoundly personal relationship with Him. It is in that intimacy in which our true self is encountered by the real Christ, that we receive the strength of His grace. If we look deeply into His grace, we discover some of its wonderful qualities:

- *Grace is unqualified, unlimited love.* It is also unmerited favor. We can never earn or deserve it. The grace that is in Christ Jesus is revealed in the cross. We are strengthened at the weakest point of our inability to atone for ourselves, justify ourselves, or exonerate ourselves. Strength cannot flow into us as long as we are burdened by our sins or failures. On a daily basis, we can allow the Holy Spirit to reassure us that we don't have to carry the weight of yesterday's mistakes. We are free from self-righteousness, from the dishonesty of the duality of pretending to be one thing on the outside, while inside we are distressed and disturbed.

- *The grace of Christ is prevenient.* The word *prevenient* means "beforehand." When used about grace, it means beforehand love, acceptance that is given before we ask for it, forgiveness offered before we seek it, Christ's choice of us before we choose to be chosen.

- *Christ's grace is also initiative.* He makes the first move. The very nature of sin is that it dulls our desire to seek forgiveness. Christ comes to us when we can't come to Him because of the bondage of guilt and self-justification. Christ never gives up on us. The very desire to seek the strength of His grace is the result of His initiation.

- *Further, Christ's grace is inexhaustible.* We simply cannot diminish the supply. He goes before us, opening doors, arranging circumstances, changing situations and people, and constantly surprising us with serendipities. Things don't work out; Christ works out things! Christ gives us exactly what we need in every moment: the assurance that we are loved, the confidence that He will bring good out of our difficulties, and the strength to do what He guides us to do in untangling our problems. There is no joy when we are worried about whether we'll have what it takes. But equally so, there is no joy to be compared to the joy we feel when we know that we are empowered by the Savior of the world. That means accepting His strength.

Why is Christ willing to love and bless us? Because there is nothing more magnetic and attractive than a person who is serenely confident of His strength. When people see and feel His strength in us, they want to know how they can find it for themselves. We are essential in Christ's strategy for reaching people around us.

Paul uses three metaphors to drive home his challenge to Timothy about being strong in the grace that is in Christ Jesus. The young leader is called to endure hardship as a good soldier of Jesus Christ, be like an athlete who plays by the rules in his training and in the race or game, and be like the farmer who partakes of the fruit of his labors. These three metaphors help us understand what we can do to receive this magnificent gift of strength for each new day.

Single-Minded Focus

The strength which is offered to us is received by those who endure hardship with the single-mindedness of a good soldier of Jesus Christ (2 Timothy 2:3) Paul reminds Timothy, and us, that strength is for the battle. Throughout his epistles, Paul talked of the warfare of the Christian against the forces of Satan, the enemies of the gospel, and the opposition of people who don't know Christ, and the stringent resistance of the defenders of the status quo. In Ephesians 6, the apostle calls us to get suited up with the armor of God for the daily battle. Often he referred to fellow Christians as soldiers of Christ. In fact, the church in Ephesus met in the home of Archippus, whom Paul called a fellow soldier. The salient point Paul makes here is that a good soldier is concerned only for pleasing the one who has enlisted him to serve. The good soldier has a focused attention on his commander and obeying his orders.

Strength is given to those whose allegiance is to Christ alone. All other people, positions, or obligations are realms in which this allegiance is lived out but are never allowed to take first place. Strength is given us to do what Christ calls us to do. We are given indefatigable courage to love, forgive, communicate hope, battle for righteousness, take stands, and serve those in need. In it all, we are soldiers under orders and answer to only one commander of our lives. We are committed to obedience, loyalty, and willingness to sacrifice. Paul reminds Timothy that no good soldier entangles himself in the affairs of this life. That's a wake-up call for most of us. So often we become so captivated with the details of daily life and the stuff of our material success.

A man who was forced to leave his home in New Orleans during Hurricane Katrina confided, "All I could take with me were a few family photos. Now, reflecting on what's important, I realize how much of my life had been focused on acquisitive accumulation of things. Now I want to get back to basics: serving Christ and paying more attention to what He orders me to do each day."

Playing by the Rules

The second metaphor Paul uses to describe those who receive supernatural strength is the athlete who competes according to the rules. There are rules for every game and every race. It is in keeping with these rules that an athlete must strive for winning but also excellence. Applied to the Christian, surely Paul meant living by the Ten Commandments and Jesus' eleventh commandment to love as He has loved us. We can be sure that the Holy Spirit will never guide us to do anything which contradicts these commandments. We run the race of discipleship reaching out for the "goal for the prize of the upward call of God in Christ Jesus" (Philippians 3:14). So Christ is the goal of our race and the strength to run it. Count Zinzendorf said about Christ, "I have one passion. It is He; it is He!"

Patient Endurance

The third metaphor in Paul's encouragement to Timothy to receive strength in Christ is the patient endurance of the hardworking farmer. The emphasis, however, catches our attention. "The hardworking farmer must be the first to partake of the crops." The toil of the farmer gives him the right to reap and enjoy the firstfruits of the crop. But what is the key truth Paul is trying to communicate to Timothy and to us? The farmer plows the field, plants the seed, waits patiently for the plant to break through the surface of the ground, cultivates the earth, removes the weeds, and then harvests the result of his labor. The metaphor teaches that we are given strength to be patient as we plant a seed of some challenge or opportunity, some problem or concern over some person and wait for the Lord's will to be done. Here's the twist: The patience the Lord provides becomes our character trait. We partake of the firstfruits of the harvest.

The Strength of Christ's Patience

If we would learn patience, Christ alone can teach us. There are many facsimiles of this character trait, but authentic lasting patience comes as a result of a deep personal relationship with Christ.

The original Greek word Paul used for patience in the list of the fruit of the Spirit is *makrothumia*. It's a compound word: *makros*—"long or far"—and *thumos*—"hot, anger, wrath or temper." Patience is "long or slow anger"—long-tempered. "Temper" is a word that describes the quality of our attitudes, the characteristic frame of our minds. Another way of putting it is that attitudes are congealed thought and the expression of those attitudes comprises our temperament. We talk about quick-tempered or even-tempered people. The fruit of the Spirit in us makes us *long*-tempered.

Another word for patience in the New Testament is *hupomone*. It reveals how we become long-tempered. *Hupomone* also is a compound word: *hupo*—"under"; *meno*— "to abide." When the Spirit of Christ abides in us, we abide under His control. We are enabled by Him to wait for His perspective and power. If we trust Him, He will guide us in how we are to react and what we are to say. Our temperament is transformed by Christ in us. Mysteriously, the transplant of His character trait of patience is planted in us and begins to grow. He reminds us of His unqualified love and forgiveness, His indefatigable patience with us in our failures, and His repeated interventions to help us. Christ never gives up on us. And as we abide under His gracious care, we discover a new power to be long-tempered, that is, patient, with ourselves and others. But the wonder of it all is that He is the patience we are able to express.

The Yoke of Christ

The process of becoming a patient person happens in the school of Christ. It takes place when we are yoked with Him. He has given us the secret of the fruit of His indwelling presence:

> Come to Me, all you who labor and are heavy-laden, and I will give you rest. Take My yoke upon you, and learn from Me; for I am gentle and lowly in heart, and you will find rest for your souls. For My yoke is easy, and My burden is light (Matthew 11:28-30).

The Lord's invitation and promise gives us four salient aspects of how to learn to be patient in His style and by His power.

Jesus Christ invites the impatient to come to Him, those who have tried to be faithful and creative and have not been able to pull it off. Only a person who has values, standards, and a vision of what life can be is impatient with himself, other people, or circumstances. In substance, He says to us, "Come to me, I understand the disappointment and frustration you feel. I know your integrity and the heartache you experience when you miss the mark. I want to give you a gift—an entirely new way to live."

The second dynamic of this verse tells how Christ proposes to impart this precious gift. He offers an exchange of yokes. Investigation into the Eastern methods of plowing helps us to understand what Jesus meant by the yoke. Mosaic law forbade an old and a young ox to be hitched together in an ordinary yoke.

The cadence of His perfect will in our lives sets the rhythm for a life of peace.

This was because the young animal could not pull his part of the burden.

The phrase "unequally yoked" comes from this. A training yoke was required by law. The heavy end of the yoke was the burden of the stronger, older beast. The experienced bovine kept the furrow straight and, under the reins of the plowman, moved forward. All the younger beast had to do was to keep parallel with the stronger animal; if it pulled away, ahead or behind, its neck would be rubbed raw in the yoke. The trainee had to give up the right to lead in order to keep pace with the trainer. The lead ox must take the lead and the responsibility for the burden. Now it begins to dawn on us what Christ meant when He offered us His yoke as a source of freedom...and patience.

Our minds leap to the implication. Christ carries the heavy end of the yoke. He pulls the burden for us. We must give up our wills to Him. Patience is developed in the school of Christ. We are yoked with Him to discover how to live with His guidance, strategy, and timing. Impatience involves running ahead, pulling off in our own direction, or stomping our feet in petulant pouting. Patience is developed through keeping a parallel pace with the Master. The cadence of His perfect will in our lives sets the rhythm for a life of peace.

We all know what it is like to be rubbed raw by our own impatience. We have all tried to accomplish our goals with only our own strength; and equally defeating, we have tried to do His work in our strength. It will not work. We become impatient when we want to do what we want, when we want it, and with whom we want it. Who has not bashed down a closed door while an open door stood nearby, with the Master inviting us to follow Him inside?

. . . .

Christ Carries Our Burdens

To be in a training yoke with Christ means several magnificent gifts are offered to us. He carries the burden! We were never created to live the Christian life on our own. The source of our strength is in surrendering our burdens to Him. As soon as we are yoked with Christ, the load is lifted. All we have to do is keep pace. Bernard of Clairvaux explained that such a yoke is a blessed burden that makes all burdens light, a yoke that bears the bearer up.

In the yoke with Christ, we can give up the responsibility of running the universe. We can have intimate communion with the Lord at all times. Our times are in His hands. He knows what He is doing. When was the last time you told Him that you knew that and completely turned over to Him the direction, desires, and duration of your life's furrow? Patience is the fruit of that yoke-union.

Thomas à Kempis said that if we want to be free to persist in our own will, then we will never be peaceful or free from care. Impatience really is breaking the first commandment. It is making ourselves a god over our own lives. It does not work. It has not since the beginning of time.

The third aspect of Matthew 11:28-30 is focused on what Jesus teaches us while we are yoked to Him. He tells us that He is "gentle and lowly in heart." The King James Version of the Bible renders it "meek and lowly." The words mean "lead-able, open to be guided, teachable, receptive."

One of the uses of the word *meek* was for an animal which had been broken and would follow the lead of the reins. An impatient person is the opposite of this. Impatience is bucking, refusing to be guided, and taking things into our own control. It is demanding that things go our way, on our schedule, regardless of cost.

The fourth aspect of Christ's salient secret for the cure of impatience is that the yoke of Christ provides rest for our souls. The Lord promised that if we want to become yokefellows with Him, we will need consistent times of rest. As the leader of our yoked-training with Him, He will not only lead the way and determine the pace, but He will also know when to stop us in our tracks. The word *rest* in this verse means refreshment. The Lord refreshes us by renewing our inner conviction that He is the source of our wisdom and guidance, and a strategic timing. It is when we are quiet that we know that He is able to do all things well and is worthy of our trust.

The Lord told the psalmist, "Be still, and know that I am God." When the psalmist followed the Lord's directive, he was able finally to write the admonition, "Wait on the LORD; be of good courage, and He shall strengthen your heart; wait, I say, on the LORD!" (Psalm 27:14). "My soul, wait silently for God alone, for my expectation is from Him" (Psalm 62:5). Note the progression: wait, receive courage, and go forward with strength. Without resting in the Lord, our impatience causes impetuousness. Our greatest errors and strained relationships come when we have lost touch with the Lord's inner guidance and wisdom.

Frederick W. Faber expressed how we must wait for God. We must wait long, meekly, in wind and wet, in the thunder and lightning, in the cold and the dark. We must wait, and He will come. But God never comes to those who do not wait.

It is in the waiting times that our most creative thoughts and plans are formulated. Instead of rushing headlong in our own impatience, the Lord is able to tell us what are the next steps and how we are to move forward in His strategy for us and the people around us.

Christ's strength gives us patience. We could never produce it on our own strength, in the quantities that are needed in our families, and our world. But we do have access to an unlimited stockpile of patience, when the fruit of the Spirit of patience gives us courage to live on His timing and act with His power. (We will consider this further in chapter 7.)

So stoke the fire and allow Christ to fuel it with the strength of His grace. Don't get out of bed until you do it. Most of all, don't leave home without Christ's strength.

. . . .

CHAPTER FOUR

Flaming
with Faithfulness

The faithfulness of Christ fuels the fires of faithfulness in us. The more we reflect on and experience His faithfulness to us in our times of need, the more we will flame with faithfulness in our character and countenance. The wondrous privilege of belonging to Christ is that we receive a character transplant and become more like Him in our attitudes and actions. And there is no greater desire than to be like the Master in faithfulness. If we had to select one of the aspects of Christ's nature as His crowning attribute, we'd probably say His faithfulness.

All the other attributes of the Savior are dependent on the immutability, unchangeableness, consistency, and constancy of His dependable faithfulness. He never acts out of character, He is never less than His grace, and He never contradicts His own nature. He will always love us; His promises are sure.

❧ ❧ ❧

If indeed, faithfulness is the crowning attribute of Christ, then it must be the crowning attribute of those who follow Him as Lord. Faithfulness is a fruit of the Spirit in us. The Lord's faithfulness is that He cannot deny Himself.

When the fire of the Spirit burns in us, we will be given the courage not to deny the Lord or the character traits He is nurturing in us. Trying to be faithful on our own strength leads to either self-righteousness or defeatism. However, the indwelling Spirit reorients our thinking about who we are. We are chosen and cherished disciples of Christ, elected to be remade in His image. Faithfulness is being true to our new self, consistent and constant in the struggles and strains of life.

In 2 Timothy 2:8-13, Paul calls Timothy, and now us, to focus on the faithfulness of Christ. Then he witnesses to the faithfulness he has been empowered to express in suffering. Finally, in the words of a hymn from the early church, the apostle attests to the indefatigable quality of Christ's faithfulness.

Survival in Suffering

In order to receive the full impact of this passage, we need to understand the particular kind of suffering Paul said he was enduring and put that into the context of his trust in the faithfulness of Christ. The word for suffer in verse 9, "I suffer trouble," also can be translated "I suffer evil." An old Greek compound is used, *kakopathō* (*kukon*—evil; *paschō*—suffer). This is a very strong word, indicating the influences of evil or Satan himself to use what happens to us to try to induce us to question God's faithfulness in the management of our lives. We become vulnerable when a physical, emotional, or relational difficulty causes us to wonder if the Lord has forgotten us. Then we have two kinds of pain to deal with: the anguish of the situation, and the anxiety over why God has allowed it.

"Why did this happen?" we ask. "What is the Lord up to in permitting this to happen to me?" we demand. A prolonged illness, relentless pain, heartbreaking grief, strained or broken relationships, misunderstanding of the motives of others, or feeling misunderstood, problems that pile up, worries that wear us down, the suffering of others—all can bring us to the edge of doubting the goodness of the Lord. We suffer the temptation to question His love for us. When we go through tough times and wonder what good can come out of what we are enduring, we find it difficult to trust the Lord. Added to all this, at times we've all been upset by the thoughtlessness, carelessness, or just plain cussedness of people. Why does God allow their derisive and divisive words and actions?

We get disappointed with God. Sometimes we are downright angry at what He has allowed to happen. Our sense of justice, mingled with a lot of pride, makes us wonder why we deserve what happens when we've done our best to serve God.

We can't be possessed by evil, but we sure can be hassled in our thinking by the diabolical mischief of Satan himself. It causes the worst kind of suffering. We become engaged in spiritual warfare. To wage that battle each day, we need to experience the faithfulness of Christ. Paul gives us several things to remember.

Remember Jesus Christ

"Remember...Jesus Christ, of the seed of David" (2:8), Paul wrote Timothy. This was the apostle's way of saying: Remember the Incarnate Christ who lived among us in human flesh. Remember the Christ who walked the dusty roads of Galilee, who healed the lame and gave sight to the blind, who came to seek and save the lost. Put yourself into the crowd who listened to Him. Hear from the lips of this pursuing, relentless, indefatigable Savior the unforgettable images of faithfulness: a father who would never give up on his younger son in the far country of rebellion or an elder son in the nearer country of self-righteousness; a shepherd who goes in search of a lost sheep; a merchant man who sells everything to purchase the pearl of great price.

Remember also the Christ who forgave those who didn't seem to deserve it, who gave *shalom* to the distressed, and communicated hope to the disheartened. Picture Jesus of Nazareth; focus your mind's eye on Him, don't take your attention off Him!

The Gospel accounts of Christ's life and ministry are an invaluable source of inspiration when we realize that how He dealt with people then, He seeks to deal with us; what He said then, echoes in our souls as if it were said to us personally today; and how He loved people then, He loves you and me today. "I cannot let you go; you belong to Me; come follow Me; I will never leave nor forsake you!"

Remember Jesus Christ Risen from the Dead

Paul goes on to encourage Timothy to remember the cross and the resurrection. Christ went to the cross out of faithfulness to the Father. He knew that the Father would be faithful to His promise to raise Him from the dead. Again, we come to the foot of the cross, the place where God's crowning attribute of faithfulness flashes forth with radiance. He had promised forgiveness and reconciliation in a way that revealed His righteous judgment of sin and His atoning forgiveness. Calvary was the site of divine faithfulness.

. . . .

The truth needs to grip us again and again. I recall a time of leading a Communion service. After the people were served the bread and wine, it was time for me to kneel and receive the sacrament myself. The man who served me was a close friend. In the formal setting of the chancel of a church, it was both surprising and very moving for him to use my name. "Lloyd, this is the body of Christ, broken for you; this is Christ's blood shed for *you!*" An unexpected thrill reverberated through me as I experienced again what I've known for 58 years, and taught and preached for 50 years. Christ died for *me.* In a very memorable moment, I remembered Christ crucified. I was at the foot of the cross and experienced fresh grace.

When we relive Calvary, we realize what an awesome revelation of God's faithfulness the resurrection was and is. Christ's resurrection was both vindication and validation of His life and death. Not only that, in Christ's resurrection death was defeated. For us who believe in Him as Lord and Savior, fear of death is gone. This life is but a small part of eternity. Our physical dying will be no more than a transition in eternal life which begins now and never ends. When we remember Christ rose from the dead, we know that no suffering can separate us from the Lord. Also, we know that one of Satan's most powerful weapons, death and fear of dying, has been wrenched from his hands. When we remember the open tomb, we claim the ultimate assurance of victory over death. We can't really live until we are sure that we are alive forever. For resurrection living, there is resurrection power that produces joy for the living of each hour.

According to My Gospel

Another reason Paul could survive in suffering was because he had a gospel. It was not audacious for him to say, "According to my gospel." Paul had an *evangel*—a gospel, good news, truth he had experienced and spent his life communicating to others. It is not an overstatement to say that the apostle Paul was the greatest human being that ever lived. After his encounter with the living Christ and his conversion, he spent 14 years in Arabia, where Christ became the center and source of his being, and previously-held tradition was transformed by experiential truth. His rich training as a Pharisee and his deep intellectual discipline was fulfilled by knowing personally the Messiah, Immanuel. Jesus Christ became Paul's purpose and passion. He had a gospel, exciting good news to share. What he wrote to the Christians at Rome might well stand as his mission statement, "When I come to you, I shall come in the fullness of the blessing of the gospel of Christ" (Romans 15:29).

The Gospel According to You

What would you say is your gospel? What is the good news according to you? We all have a gospel, however weak or strong. What Christ means to us personally and our personal application of His message, death, resurrection, and reigning power to all of the exigencies of life become our gospel. People around us are reading the gospel according to you or me all the time. How we have thought through what we believe about the faithfulness of Christ will determine how we survive in tough times. In the midst of physical pain, emotional turmoil, relational trauma, is not the time to work out what we believe about how the Lord will strengthen us. Now is the time!

The reason I'm so captivated by Paul's second epistle to Timothy is because in it I can read the apostle's last will and testament, his distilled theological thinking applied to excruciating suffering there in prison. All that he had preached to others worked for him in the last days of his life. Paul held firm intellectual convictions about the absolutely reliable faithfulness of Christ and was sustained by these beliefs. His gospel did not let him down, nor will ours.

Freedom in the Fetters

Paul had freedom in spite of the fetters that bound him. "I suffer trouble as an evildoer, even to the point of chains; but the Word of God is not chained" (verse 9). The apostle could endure the chains because he knew that the Word of God was being spread through him and Christians throughout the then-known world. It has been said that many of the guards to whom Paul was chained became converted, and that they had to be rotated off that duty assignment by the Roman government. Imagine being chained to Paul! His contagious communication of the Word of God's faithfulness in Christ was so strong that guards who were chained to him for six hours at a time could not resist the de-

> *We may be chained by some adversity, but the spread of Christ's love can never be chained.*

sire to know Christ personally. Paul also knew that no one could ever stop the spread of the gospel.

It is a humbling but also a liberating perspective to know that our lives are a vital part of Christ's forward movement in the world. We may be chained by some adversity, but the spread of Christ's love can never be chained. He is sovereign of the Kingdom, and ultimately never can be defeated.

The Inspiration of Others

Another source of strength in suffering for Paul was the assurance that what he was going through would be an inspiration for those who were already among the elect, but would obtain salvation. "Therefore," he wrote Timothy, "I endure all things for the sake of the elect, that they also may obtain the salvation which is in Christ Jesus with eternal glory" (2:10). This statement is power-packed with the faithfulness of both Christ and Paul. Paul had a profound trust in the Lord's prevenient choice and subsequent call of those who had become Christians. Those who were already among those chosen by the Lord would see in Paul's courageous endurance what trust in Christ's faithfulness can do in the midst of difficult times.

Nothing Is Wasted

Don't miss what all this means for you and me. Nothing is wasted. Even our tough times can be used to show others what Christ's faithfulness has done to give us courage. People are watching...be sure of that. They want to know that the Lord's faithfulness does make a difference in the problems and perplexities of life.

The Lord will use what happens to us to help us communicate His strength through us. Over the 50 years of my ministry, I've learned that either during or soon after a time of discovering the faithfulness of Christ in some adversity or blessing, I will be given the opportunity to empathize with and encourage someone who is facing a similar situation. So much so, that whenever I go through a challenging time, I say, "Who will it be this time, Lord?" And then I meet the person, receive a phone call from someone, or get a friend on my mind, and I know that what the Lord has helped me face and experience of His grace in adversity will be used for His glory and the growth of someone He's chosen to meet Him and be strengthened by Him through me. It's awesome how He works!

We are relieved of the burden of convincing people of Christ's faithfulness. Our responsibility is to share what we know from our own experience. And the very things we go through become contact points in our witness. People will hear because the Lord has elected them to be believers, called them to receive what we say about the real-to-life discoveries we've made, and calls them to respond. So get ready!

My Own Experience

During the past three years I have experienced in a personal way the faithfulness of Christ in loss and new beginnings. On March 13, 2003, I left my post as Chaplain of the United States Senate to care for my wife of 52 years, Mary Jane. On April 1, 2003, she graduated to heaven after a long illness, culminating a year of hospitalization in 2002 and into 2003.

All through that last year, Christ intervened with amazing faithfulness. In Washington, during the first six months, and then during the last six months in Los Angeles, friends rallied and were on time, in time with expressions of the Lord's care. Letters of love and encouragement were sent by President Bush, Don Rumsfeld, Sandra Day O'Connor, senators and staff of the Senate, along with notes from friends all over the world. One day, Bill Frist, eminent cardiologist and surgeon, and leader in the Senate (later majority leader), was called in as a consultant during one of Mary Jane's emergency operations. He canceled all his appointments, raced across Washington, gave his expertise on the surgery, and then sat with me for six hours. Mary Jane was given several months more because of this successful surgery.

When it seemed right to medevac Mary Jane from Washington to Los Angeles, to give her time with the children and grandchildren, the cost was $25,000. My reserves were already drained. Just before the day of the trip, my friend Ron Glosser called to say that he and four other friends had provided the fare for the aircraft, the cost for medical personnel, and all the added expenses. The five men all felt led by Christ to respond to this need.

All through the weeks and months from October 2002, to April 1, 2003, Mary Jane was on a breathing machine that enabled her to breathe through a tracheal tube. She could communicate only with a slight whisper and by writing notes. So often, she would affirm that Christ was with her in the suffering. Often during that year, several times she lost consciousness, and I thought she might not regain it, but repeatedly she returned to be able to express love for her family and friends. The excruciating pain persisted, and the hourly suction of her lungs was traumatic to her and those of us who watched. Finally, one day in March 2003, she was rushed from Barlow Respiratory Hospital to Cedars Hospital for an emergency operation because of a hole in her esophagus. After repeated efforts to place and keep in place an ever-enlarged stent in the hole, the doctors told my children and me that her days were numbered. She said she was ready. A week later, on April 1, she joined the company of heaven.

All through the months of grief recovery, I would cry out to Christ for fresh power to face the future. I still remember poorly cooked meals I cooked and ate standing up at the kitchen counter. The long nights and lonely days prompted me to pray for healing of grief and loneliness. Soon, my life filled up with speaking engagements, travel, and writing.

I still remember the day, over a year after Mary Jane's graduation to heaven, that I felt a profound change within me. I had asked the Lord to heal me and give me enthusiasm for the present and excitement for His plans for my life. He was faithful. One day, the burden of grief was lifted, and expectation for the future flooded my being.

About this time, I saw a lovely woman named Doris Sumner, whom Mary Jane and I had known as a casual friend at a golf club years before. In a passing, brief visit, I learned that her husband, Jim, had died. We exchanged sympathies for both of our losses. When Doris walked away, I sensed Christ's stirring an inner sense that somehow Doris would play an important part in my future. I had no idea then just how important. Not knowing what the Lord was indicating, I wrote out Doris's name on a piece of paper and placed it prominently for a daily prayer reminder.

Six months later, I called Doris to ask her to accompany me to a community social function where I was to give an invocation. She accepted, and then I learned two very significant things: Doris's husband, Jim, and Mary Jane, had died on the same day—April 1, 2003. Jim had suffered a prolonged illness before his death. The other thing I learned during that phone call was that the night before Doris had gone to the opening at the Los Angeles Billy Graham Crusade in the Rose Bowl in Pasadena. When I opened the Crusade, Doris and her friends were seated far from the podium, but could see everything on a large television screen. When I appeared, Doris tells me she felt some kind of stirring similar to what I had experienced six months before. There had been no personal contact during that time. Now on the phone, here I was asking her to go with me to a December 1, 2004, Christmas ball.

. . . .

—

That evening together began a wonderful friendship that soon turned into a courtship, and a proposal of marriage. Doris and I both felt the Lord's arrangement of our relationship. In hundreds of ways, we could see His faithful hand guiding us. On April 9, 2005, we were married. Three senators came to participate in the service and ask the questions usually asked by the clergyman in the giving of the bride. Bill Frist asked, "Who gives Doris to be married to Lloyd?" Her family responded, "We do!" Connie Mack followed with, "Who approves of this marriage?" And my family answered, "We do!" Jon Kyl then asked, "And who will pray for Doris and Lloyd as they are made one in marriage?" And the congregation responded, "We all will!"

The whole service, led by six clergy friends, and attended by loved ones and friends, was an expression of praise to the Lord for His faithfulness in all that both Doris and I have been through in recent years, and then gratitude for the serendipity of unexpected joy in our new life together. The hymn sung during the wedding service was "Great Is Thy Faithfulness." There were tears in our eyes and thanksgiving in our hearts as we held hands and sang with strong conviction, "Thou changest not, Thy compassions, they fail not; as Thou hast been, Thou forever wilt be…Thine own dear presence to cheer and to guide; strength for today and bright hope for tomorrow, blessings all mine, with ten thousand beside! Great is Thy faithfulness! Great is Thy faithfulness! Morning by morning new mercies I see. All I have needed Thy hand hath provided; great is Thy faithfulness, Lord, unto me!"[6]

In our version, Doris and I sang, and continue to sing, "Great is Thy faithfulness, Lord, unto *us!*" Now, after the first year together, we gratefully affirm the years past and joyfully anticipate new evidences of the Lord's faithfulness in the unfolding future.

Here is a poem to Doris I wrote and shared at our wedding reception.

> *A lassie, a leddy, a ferlie, a love*
> *Whose loveliness I hold gently like a dove,*
> *One whose smile lights up a room*
> *And makes my heart go zoom;*
> *One whose laughter warms my soul*
> *And makes me happy, carefree, and whole;*
> *One whose bright mind is so stimulating*
> *And makes conversations scintillating;*
> *One whose beauty is an awesome delight*
> *And in my mind's eye she's never out of sight;*
> *One whose tender touch is satisfying*
> *And makes just holding hands electrifying;*
> *One who is radiant with Christ's passion,*
> *And is fully alive in every fashion;*

. . . .

> *One who makes it such a joy to be together*
> *I can imagine loving her now and forever.*
> —*Your Scottish Admirer*

I have shared this experience so that readers who have read my books through the years, as well as you who are new friends reading for the first time, will know the impact of Christ's faithfulness in my pilgrimage.

Christ's Faithfulness to His Nature

Paul concludes his own witness to Timothy about Christ's faithfulness by quoting what must have been a hymn in the early church. It affirms Christ's faithfulness to His own nature. The hymn is arranged into four couplets, which are followed by one of the most reassuring lines of Scripture.

In the first couplet, the central truth of Christ's cross and our own cross is boldly declared: "If we died with Him, we shall also live with Him" (verse 11). The cycle of death to self, resurrection of a new self, and the regeneration of the new self into Christ's likeness is asserted. Romans 6:8 proclaims this same basic truth, "If we died with Christ, we believe we shall also live with Him." In Galatians 2:20, Paul had witnessed to his own experience of this triumphant transition from crucifixion of self and the reorientation of the self to be a postresurrection home of the living Christ:

> I have been crucified with Christ; it is no longer I
> who live, but Christ lives in me; and the life which
> I now live in the flesh I live by faith in the Son of
> God, who loved me and gave Himself for me.

All of this is on this side of heaven.

The second couplet goes on to declare, "If we endure, we shall also reign with Him" (verse 12). All during the ups and downs of life, with the liberating conviction and assurance of Christ's faithfulness in life and death, we shall live with Him in the company of heaven forever. In heaven, we will see the plan for the culmination of history and join with Him in intercession before the Father for those whom we have left on earth. We will worship with the company of angels and archangels, the saints of the ages, around the Father's throne. We will know the joy of heaven, the eternal home of the loved and forgiven.

However, the next couplet is startling: "If we deny Him, He will also deny us." This is a bracing statement of reality. A persistent denial of Christ as our Lord produces a dreadful result. Saying "No!" to His Lordship, His daily guidance, and His hourly inspiration, eventually withers our wills to the point that it is difficult to say "Yes." We can say "No" so long that eventually we aren't able to say "Yes." This couplet repeats the disturbing truth of Christ's own statement during His earthly ministry,

> Whoever confesses Me before men, him I will also confess before My Father who is in heaven. But whoever denies Me before men, him I will also deny before My Father who is in heaven (Matthew 10:32-33).

This is a realistic statement of the assumption that whoever has not acknowledged Christ as Lord in this life, probably would not want to go to heaven where all they do is glorify Christ, and with Him, worship the Father. Neglect is as serious as actual denial. Why? Because confession of Christ as Lord and Savior opens the gates of heaven.

In the light of that, we wonder about the meaning of the next couplet: "If we are faithless, He remains faithful" (verse 13). I think this means the lack of trust in Christ in the daily challenges and opportunities of life. There is a difference between primary faith in our confession of Christ as Lord, and pertinacious—resolutely unyielding—faith that expects and joyfully receives the interventions of His grace. This means that even though those of us who believe in Christ vacillate in our discipleship and resist His control of our lives in specifics, He does not change. Why? Because He cannot deny Himself. Christ will never deny His own nature, which is to persist in His faithfulness even when we try to run our own lives.

This is the best assurance of His faithfulness we can find: The Lord cannot deny Himself. He must be true to His own nature; He will never contradict His promises; He always will be consistent. Even when we are faithless, shake our fist in rebellion, turn on our heels, and try to run away from Him, He is faithful. And because He is, all other aspects of His nature—love, joy, peace, patience, kindness, and goodness—never fail. Once we acknowledge that we belong to Him, He will always find a way to bring us back if we stray from Him.

The Fires of Faithfulness

If indeed faithfulness is the crowning attribute of Christ, then it must be the crowning aptitude of our lives. When the Spirit bellows the fires within us, we flame with faithfulness. We are given blazing courage not to deny Christ or the new character trait of faithfulness He is stoking up in us. Once more for emphasis: The result is that the Lord's faithfulness is implanted into our character; the crowning attribute of the Lord is cloned in us. We can survive, even thrive, in the stress and suffering of life. All because the Lord is faithful to help us and makes us faithful.

CHAPTER FIVE

Warming Up the Frozen Chosen

The frozen chosen. Nice people, good people. Often productive, successful people. Many are efficient, generous people. Some are members of churches and are patriotic citizens.

These are chosen people who have not yet chosen to be chosen. They are all around us in our family, among our friends, in our community organizations, in our country clubs, in our favorite coffee shops.

They all have one need in common: They need to be melted by the fires of passion for life blazing in us.

Unless I miss my guess, more than a few of you who are reading this book just cringed. You have braced yourself for a precipitous chapter on personal evangelism. Strange, isn't it, how reluctant most of us are to communicate our faith. We can talk about current events, politics, sports, the stock market, our health, and pain we may have experienced in physical disabilities. However, we get lockjaw when there is an opportunity to share what Christ has done for us. We don't want to appear to be fanatics or religious nuts.

And yet we'd all have to admit that when there was only a red ember in the white ash of our burned-out quest for meaning in our own lives, someone cared for us and in the most natural, unpretentious, impious, nonjudgmental way, helped put the bellows on the hearth of our hearts. We dare not do less for others who have not yet accepted how much the Lord loves them. Our task is to find a way to communicate our caring concern for them.

Caring Is Everything

When the great mystic and philosopher Baron von Hügel lay dying, his niece noticed that his lips were moving. She could not hear what he was trying to say, so she put her ear close to his mouth. What she heard was this: "Caring is everything; nothing matters but caring." I would agree. Caring is friendship in action. It is a precious gift we can offer others.

At the close of a retreat some time ago, we sang the refrain, "He careth for you, He careth for you. Through sunshine or shadow, He careth for you." Then we turned to the people around us and sang it again changing the pronoun from "He" to "I." Tears streamed down many faces as people sang what they felt so deeply: "I care for you."

The result of this moving expression of care was that several people at the retreat who were among the frozen chosen, felt deeply loved. Subsequently, on long walks or over meals, the caring melted the resistance of these people and by the end of the last day of the retreat they were led through the steps of turning their lives over to Christ. Those frozen chosen chose to be chosen!

This chapter is about how the fire in us can be used to

> *The fire in us can be used to not only warm, but ignite the fires of faith in others.*

not only warm, but ignite the fires of faith in others. What is required in us is personal, practical caring for the people we long to reach.

Being Passionate Communicators

A while ago, I was sitting in a restaurant having lunch. I overheard a woman in the next booth exclaim, "Listen, I couldn't care less!" I turned around and said, "About what?" Her embarrassed reply was, "It's none of your business!"

Afterward, I reflected on those oft-repeated words, "I couldn't care less." They are a way of expressing dismissive disdain. And yet, often I think people really mean "I wish I didn't care so much." For us the phrase is a double entendre: It really means we realize we can never care enough.

Those who share the high calling of living their faith with passion, stand first at the foot of the cross and look into the face of the Savior, then beside an empty tomb with *"sursum corda"* ringing in our souls, and then in the Upper Room witnessing the miracle of Pentecost and experiencing the power of the Spirit. We say, "How could I ever care less?" Less than the Lord has cared, less than He cares for us and the frozen chosen we would like to warm with the fires of a passionate faith.

Now we are ready to turn our attention to what it means to be passionate communicators of our faith to others. At first, we face the etymological challenge of the misuse of the word *passion* in our day. We begin with the false, exclusive attachment to sex. Fortunately, the English definition broadens the scope: "Strong feelings of love, anger or desire." We are still on the surface. We press deeper to discover the meaning of passion in the Greek New Testament. *Paschō* is directly related to Christ's suffering on the cross. Acts 1:3 is a fulcrum text: "He [Christ] also presented Himself alive after His *suffering by* many infallible proofs." Here *pathein*— passion, or suffering—is the second aorist active of *paschō*. *Pathein* is also used in Acts 17:3 and 26:23 for Christ's suffering—His expiatory and vicarious sacrifice for the sins of the world.

But press on! The word passion in New Testament Greek also is used for the suffering of the first century followers of Christ. Paul goes so far as to use the compound *sunpaschōman,* to suffer with Christ, in Romans 8:16-17:

> The Spirit Himself bears witness with our spirit that we are children of God, and if children, then heirs—heirs of God and joint heirs with Christ, if indeed we suffer with Him, that we may also be glorified together.

Suffering with Christ is the secret to being glorified with Him.

Allow me to suggest an authentic definition of passion. It is suffering love produced in us by the Holy Spirit, inspiring a fresh experience of Christ's grace in our souls, and then producing profound empathy for the people to whom we want to witness, expressed with incisive intellectual truth, intense feeling, and intrepid enthusiasm.

In other words, sharing our faith with passion is allowing our minds and hearts to become crucibles for compounding our own experience of Christ's unqualified, unmerited, unfettered love for our suffering—and our identification with the sometimes expressed, but often hidden, suffering of other people. Robert Burns was right, "If each man's internal care were written on his brow, those who have our envy would have our pity now."

When we have listened to the deepest needs and urgent questions of people, we "cannot care less" than to respond. We share our faith with passion when people's anguish is on our hearts, when we realize that without Christ they are lost now and for eternity, and when we enter into the problems and perplexities, the agonies and ecstasies of loved ones, friends, people at work, and in our communities.

The Source of Our Passion

Christ Himself is the source of this passion. We can say with Charles Spurgeon, "We have a great need for Christ, and a great Christ for our needs!" We have one passion. It is He!

The content of the gospel is the source of the stirring convictions that stimulate our passion. We need to live in the ethos of the primitive church and its essential message focused on the preexistent Christ, the divine Word of God, the Incarnate Son, the suffering, crucified Savior, the risen Victor over Satan and death, the triumphant, reigning Lord, and the baptizer with the Holy Spirit. Oscar Cullman said, "It is the *present* Lordship of Christ inaugurated by His resurrection and exaltation to the right hand of God that is the center of the faith of primitive Christianity."

It is also to be the center of our faith and life. We come from our times of study and prayer with the undeniable conviction that what happened to the followers and disciples of Christ, mysteriously, but undeniably, can be recapitulated in our own minds and hearts today.

"Good Morning, Mr. President"

There's a wonderful story told about Lincoln's biographer, Carl Sandburg, that exemplifies what needs to be our acute awareness of the presence of Christ. Sandburg became so immersed in his study of Lincoln that he thought of little else. The people in the town where he studied and wrote decided to test his concentration on Abe. They noted that the historian went to breakfast the same time and place each day. So they dressed up the tallest man in town as Abraham Lincoln and had him walk down the street just in time to meet Sandburg as he walked to the restaurant. Everyone watched and listened as the two met. Without blinking an eye, or slowing his pace, Sandburg tipped his hat and said, "Good morning, Mr. President." He was so engulfed in his Lincolnology that he was not surprised to see Lincoln on his own street!

In a much more profound and realistic way, we need to be so immersed in the actual presence and power of Christ in our own relationship with Him that our friendship and fellowship with Him radiates on our countenances and pulsates through our words.

'Twas not just the words you spoke
To you, so clear, to me, so dim
But 'twas that when you spoke
You brought a sense of Him
In your eyes He beckoned me
And in your smile His love was spread
Until I lost sight of you
And saw the Lord instead![7]

Being Useful to Him

When we have a passion for life, we impact the lives of people around us. The warmth of the fire within us warms the people who need Christ. Our task is to melt the resistance of those who are chosen by God but who are still frozen.

How shall we communicate our faith? What is effective witness? It's a concern we all share.

Paul's advice to Timothy gives us what to avoid and what to do. Timothy and his fellow Christian workers were to avoid arguments about words that ruin hearers. The word for ruin in the Greek is *katastrophe*. We've all seen the wrong kind of witnessing that majors in the minor of pet theories or secondary issues.

The kind of witnesses God approves of and who have no need to be ashamed of their methods are those who are what Paul calls, "rightly dividing the word of truth."

Checking the Greek verb for "rightly dividing" helps us avoid a lot of misinterpretations of this verse that have been offered through the centuries. The verb is *orthotoneō*. It means "to cut straight" and is used only here in the New Testament and twice in the Septuagint, the Greek translation of the Old Testament. These two old Septuagint verses in which *orthotoneō* is used are in Proverbs. The first is 3:6: "He shall direct your paths"; the second is 11:5: "The righteousness of the blameless will direct his way aright."

So "rightly dividing the word of truth" does not mean cutting it up into little pieces, as Calvin suggested, but to cut a path in a straight direction—or as Chrysostom translated it, "driving a straight furrow in your proclamation of the truth."

The Heart of the Truth for the Heart of the Need

The challenge of the passionate communicator is to cut straight through to the heart of the need with the heart of the truth. The metaphor is extended to include clearing the way for a person to come to Christ. This kind of sharing of our faith requires that we know the needs of the people to whom we would communicate. People are like islands: You have to row around them until you know where to land. Sharing our faith requires caring relationships. Jim Rayburn, who started Young Life, called it "earning the right to be heard." That means involvement, listening with care, serving with sensitivity. It also demands affirmation of the person, with genuine empathy.

. . . .

Friendship may seem like a lightweight word for personal sharing of our faith, but that's exactly what opens up people to what we have to say. Once we know the heart of a person, we can draw on the Scriptures and illustrate with our own experience of how God helped us in a similar kind of need or challenge or question. Eventually, we are given the opportunity to cut straight through to a person's need for a personal relationship with Christ. The authenticity of what Christ means to us will establish our credentials to help a person confess Christ as Lord and Savior, surrender his or her life to Him, and receive His transforming Spirit.

Our Confidence

The confidence of the Christian communicator is "nevertheless the solid foundation of God stands, having this seal: 'The Lord knows those who are His,' and 'Let everyone who names the name of Christ depart from iniquity'" (2 Timothy 2:19). This gives us the courage of some very strong convictions:

- The Lord has gone before us in preparing people.

- Our task is being prepared to communicate with those whom He has prepared. The congruity of our walk and our talk will speak as loudly as what we say.

- There is power in personal vulnerability, freshness, and vitality.

The Useful Vessel

In the parable that follows in 2:20-23, that of the useful vessel, Paul conjures a fascinating picture. In a great and stately mansion, the master of the house maintains all sorts of vessels. Some are for use in the kitchen; others are used to serve the master. He treasures the costly gold and silver vessels used at his table. The surprising twist of Paul's metaphorical parable is that, when cleansed, the master will use the earthenware vessels, cherishing them as he does those of gold and silver.

As in any parable, we dare not get sidetracked on the secondary details. A parable is to have one main point, without distracting subplots. So, what is the one truth Paul was communicating? Simply that the Master (capital M) uses earthenware vessels like you and me, and treats us like gold and silver vessels. The salient thing is that when we are cleansed and sanctified, we become useful to the Master, Christ our Lord, and are prepared for every good work.

The Lord Needs Us

We can't delve into this passage without being reminded of the password used in preparation for Jesus' triumphal entry into Jerusalem. In keeping with Zechariah 9:9, Jesus needed a colt or donkey to ride. He sent His disciples into a village, telling them that they would find a colt. They were to bring it to Him. When asked why they were taking it, the prearranged password, "the Lord has need of it," would signal to the owner that it was to be released to Jesus.

The astounding thing about our calling is, the Lord has need of us. We are crucial to His plans, and the password for our life of being a passionate communicator is, "The Lord has need of it." It is by the Master's choice that earthenware utensils like you and me are treated as gold and silver.

Ephesians 2:10 also comes to mind:

> We are His workmanship, created in Christ Jesus
> for good works, which God prepared beforehand
> that we should walk in them.

We were created to be useful to the Master. And 2 Corinthians 4:7 drives home the point: "We have this treasure in earthen vessels, that the excellence of the power may be of God and not of us." We hold the treasure of the gospel in our clay pot lives (sometimes cracked pots). The wonder of it all is that He chooses to use us.

Servant Leaders

In light of what we have seen, we are ready to ask the penetrating question: Now that we have been chosen, cleansed, and set apart for the Master's use, can it be said of us that we are useful to Him and prepared to do the good works He has prepared for each of us to do? Not unless we follow Paul's exhortation that follows in verse 22: "Flee also youthful lusts; but pursue righteousness, faith, love, peace with those who call on the Lord out of a pure heart." The word for "youthful lusts" means self-assertion, selfish ambition, headstrong obstinacy, arrogance. These proclivities are not limited to youth! Whether young or old, we are challenged to pursue righteousness, faith, love, and peace as gentle (leadable, guidable, moldable) servants of the Master.

The point for our application here is that effective communicators think of themselves as servant leaders. When we serve people rather than demanding that we be served, we will be given the opportunity to share what Christ means to us.

The grace we have received is not for ourselves alone, but for the needs of others. We exist to share with others the abundant and eternal life we have been given. The term "life" is used 36 times in the New Testament as a synonym for Christ and for the Christian faith. It is one of the great names given to Christ; it is used by Him to describe who He is and what He came to do; it is a composite term to dramatize what happens to a person who comes to know Him; and it is a designation of a distinctive quality of relationship we share with fellow believers. Living this new life without reservation in all of our relationships, celebrating the Lord of life in all things, and sharing what it means truly to be alive with power and contagion as a result—is the central calling that grips us.

. . . .

The admonition given by the angel to Peter, John, and the other apostles when they were released from prison communicates the content and commission for sharing our faith with others. "Go stand in the Temple and speak to the people all the words of this life" (Acts 5:20). The English Standard Bible catches even more of the verve of the imperative: "Go and stand in the Temple and speak to the people all the words of this Life."

But, for a simple definition of communicating our faith to others, I like *The Good News for Modern Man* version: "Go and tell people all about this new life."

Press your ear to the New Testament; listen to the apostolic preaching; observe the early church alive; behold what happened after Pentecost; feel the power of the living Christ picking up His ministry where he left off at the ascension— the stirring note of new life. That's the dominant theme, the message that turned the world upside down. Paul and the apostles told people all about this new life, and what they shared was validated by the life they lived.

Chosen and Appointed

It was Pentecost that set ablaze the red ember in the white ash of memory in those assembled in the Upper Room. They were ablaze with more than a memory of an historical figure; Christ Himself was their life. And He had given them a mighty mandate: "You did not choose

Me, but I chose you and appointed you that you should go and bear [much] fruit" (John 15:16).

How amazing! The call to be reproductive in communicating the life they had found was not dependant on them. Our Lord wants us to realize that it is not our adequacy or even our potential, but only His call and commission which qualifies us. This is the first essential of effective communication of our faith. We are not worthy,

> *We become concerned to share life with others...because we cannot remain silent about a life that has healed us and made us whole.*

and never shall be. Before we were ready, prepared, capable, adequate, Christ called us and appointed us. That's the core of the gospel—Even "while we were yet sinners" (KJV).

> *Let me no more my comfort draw*
> *From my frail hold on Thee,*
> *In this alone rejoice,*
> *Thy mighty grasp on me.*[0]

The confusion of our minds must be broken through so that we can begin to see things as they are—Christ as He really is, ourselves as we really are. The liberating revelation must be such that at one time it shows us the truth and makes it possible for us to be honest about it. We know that

Christ has called us, appointed us, and we belong to Him in spite of what we have been or are.

This is the source of the winsome freedom which becomes the attractive ambience of our communication. We become concerned to share life with others—not because we must, but because we may; not to justify ourselves, but because we cannot remain silent about a life that has healed us and made us whole.

Called for a Purpose

Therefore, we have been called for a purpose—to bear fruit. Jesus used the profound image of the vine and the branch, and gave a liberating secret about the source of the life we are called to communicate. I believe the fruit He seeks us to bear is in the reproduction of our faith in others.

Christ is decisive in telling us that there are two kinds of branches: the one bears fruit and is pruned to bear more fruit; the other bears no fruit and is cut off and burned. The disciples knew about vines and branches. They knew about the drastic pruning process which was essential to the production of fruit. Outside the Temple in Jerusalem, there was a gigantic golden vine over the entrance to the sanctuary to remind the worshipers that Israel was the branch of the vine. It is in this context that Jesus gave the secret of fruitful communication: He is the vine; only in contact with Him do we receive the power to bear fruit.

Whoever "remains in me, and I in him…will bear much fruit" (NIV). What Christ seems to be saying is that He is the evangelist. Paul caught the essence of this in Ephesians 2:10. He talks about walking in the things God has prepared. In other words, the things we do in obedience to Him, are already prepared. They are prepared in the sense not only that He tells us what to do, but that He is doing them through us. Christ is at work!

There is one evangel, one evangelist; our task is to be channels for Christ Himself to do His work with people. We are to communicate the dynamic that Christ is Lord of all. Our task is not to force people to make Him their Lord. He is that already. Faith is accepting what has always been true. We are to help people accept the love that has been there all along. In becoming a Christian, we accept the fact that we are loved and forgiven, and open ourselves to His loving Spirit.

"If you remain in me and my words remain in you, ask whatever you wish" (John 15:7 NIV). Prayer begins with our Lord. He places within us the desire to communicate His love to some particular person. When we ask Him, it is not our task to convince Him of a person's need. He knows that already, and has prompted us to pray. Our concern is to be so deeply engrossed in moment-by-moment prayer that we sense the movement of His guiding Spirit to those people who are next on His agenda for us to share His life. We do not have to press the Lord into loving a person. That is true already. But what we do need is to get into the rhythm of His guidance so that we are ready for those whom He has made ready.

"By this My Father is glorified, that you bear much fruit" (John 15:8). The glory of the Lord is the manifestation of the Lord in the fruit He produces through us. The fruit he produces *in* us is what He wants to produce *through* us. I believe the fruit of the indwelling Christ is ministry to other people who receive a taste of the new life in relationship with us. When the Lord lives in us, He manifests Himself by making us more like Him in our character; we meet Him in communion with others where He is the source of unity and fellowship; we communicate with others to reproduce in them the reality we have found; and we join with Him in His work in society to bring justice and freedom for all people.

Loving, Listening, Caring, Sharing

The secret is entering into deep, caring relationships with people in which the new life is modeled and mediated. It is communicating life in the crucible of identification. This is what Jesus meant when He reminded His disciples of the way He had loved them. He pointed to His death as a supreme act of self-giving.

Christ has called us to die to our own selfish plans, schedules, privacy, and comfort. "The greatest love a man can have for his friends is to give his life for them" (John 15:13, my paraphrase). It is a person-centric involvement in the context of total concern for a person's life. It is not hit-and-run conceptualism in which we blast into a person's life, spew out theoretical concepts of salvation, wrench a decision from him or her, and move on to new ego trips. The issue of our time is the issue of finding ways of communicating with people who have heard the language and traditions of religion and have bypassed them as irrelevant to their lives. A freshness, a sparkle, is needed if we are to reach the pagan, post-Christian world in which we live. John Masefield put it this way:

> *The bolted door had broken in*
> *I knew that I had done with sin*
> *To brother all the souls on earth.*

Jesus' strategy of communicating our faith is for us to be to others what He has been to us. He loved His disciples in the way He had been loved by the Father. Now they were to love each other and the people He gave them; just as He had loved them. Amy Carmichael once wrote,

> *No wound? No scar?*
> *Yet, as the Master so shall the servant be*
> *And pierced are the feet that follow Me;*
> *But thine are whole: can he have followed far*
> *Who has no scar?*

. . . .

Sharing our faith is loving, listening, caring, and sharing. The great gift of the indwelling Spirit burning within us is the capacity of accepting, affirming love. It's the delight a person comes to feel about himself when he is with us. This is the ambience in which a person can see himself as he is and what could happen to him if he allowed Christ to manage his life. When people are loved, they are free to talk about themselves, their dreams, hopes, fears, frustrations, and disappointments. That's where remedial listening comes in. If we truly trust that Christ is present and His love is already at work in a person, we can listen lovingly as he talks about his life.

Listen, can you hear the plea of the people around you? Seneca echoed it long ago and died by his own hand: "Listen to me for a day, an hour, a moment, lest I expire in my terrible wilderness, my lonely silence. O, God, is there no one to listen?"

When Helen Keller spoke of her soul's sudden awakening, she said, "Somehow, the mastery of language was revealed to me, I knew that water meant that wonderful, cool something that was flowing over my hand." Ann Sullivan had matched sounds with feelings. That's what communicating our faith is all about: identifying the relationship of the deep inner needs of people with the refreshing healing of Christ's love. When people sense what Christ has done in us, they can feel what it might be like for them. Not concepts alone, but communion; not rationalizing, but relationalizing—that's authentic communication.

One of the most exciting things that I see in our time of history is what our Lord is doing in the lives of church people who have been agnostic Christians for years. There is a fantastic ferment in the Body of Christ today, and I believe it is happening through people who have come to a fresh experience of our Lord's indwelling power. These are the people who have been effective in reaching those who are among the frozen chosen.

Gentle and Humble Communicators

These on-fire communicators are distinguished by gentleness and humility. Paul concludes this section of his second letter to Timothy with a reminder of the qualities of a servant-communicator (2:24-26). They don't quarrel with people, but are gentle to all, sharing their faith with patience and remaining humble when there is opposition. The Greek word for *gentleness* means moldable and leadable; the word for patience, as we noted earlier, means to "remain under." Applied to the role of a communicator, we are called to be sensitive to the Spirit's guidance of when and how to talk to others about Christ and to take in stride that there may be opposition. We are to keep on trying because of the life or death urgency. For Paul, sharing our faith is so that people "may come to their senses and escape the snare of the devil, having been taken captive by him to do his will" (verse 26).

Again, Paul sounds a battle cry for spiritual warfare. The urgency for warming the frozen chosen is so they may not be captive of the Neutralizer, who relentlessly seeks to raid the ranks of dull, bland religious people, and keep them frozen. The Lord wants to recruit us to help others claim their status as loved and forgiven people.

Allow me to conclude this chapter with some practical action steps.

1. Pray that the Lord will make you aware of at least six frozen chosen people He has put on your agenda.

2. Pray for these people daily. Ask the Lord to help you understand their needs and affirm their potential.

3. Pray for openings the Lord will arrange to care for them and serve them in practical ways that will strengthen the bond of friendship.

4. Listen to these people attentively, so that you will know when to respond with a personal sharing that directly meets the needs they have confided to you.

Cut a straight furrow!

CHAPTER SIX

Quelling the Fire-Quenchers

W ell, that's just the way he is!"
"She's always acted that way!"

Often we hear these accommodations of eccentric or egregious behavior. Even among Christians—members, leaders, and clergy of the contemporary church—we put up with a lot of personality proclivities and character disorders. We wring our hands in consternation while tolerating un-Christlike actions or attitudes. We do this in the name of acceptance, we think.

But there is a deeper reason. All of us know of weaknesses in our own personalities that we perpetuate or resist changing.

Also, in an effort to not be judgmental, we allow people to drift along with the same relational habits they had when they began the Christian life. With too large a measure of self-indulgence, we say, "Well, I'm only human! What do you expect—perfection?"

When we consistently resist making an honest personality and character inventory and reject being changed, we become fire-quenchers: We quench the fire of the Holy Spirit within us and in others. Our behavior can keep us from being on-fire, radiant Christians. The way we act can pour cold water on the fire of enthusiasm, excitement, and expectation in others.

Often, we hear in conversation or read in the newspapers about a previously respected leader's misbehavior in moral issues, ethics, or integrity. Hardly a day goes by without some business leader being exposed for dishonesty. Political leaders often make the headlines for infractions of the rules or for charges of misconduct. The clergy are not exempt. When unresolved personality disorders cause a behavior pattern that contradicts his or her vows, we are distressed. Then we are confronted with what's happening to people in our own circle of friends. "What's this world coming to?" we ask. Maybe things have always been this bad, but we didn't have the media for instant replay.

The Stressmongers

People whose behavior or personality or character traits contradict their faith cause stress in themselves, and certainly, in the lives of people around them. I call them stressmongers. In Scotland, someone who works in a fish market is called fishmonger; or a hardware store, an iron-monger. A monger is a purveyor of something. Stressmongers are those who spread stress wherever they go.

Paul wrote Timothy that, "In the last days, perilous times will come" (2 Timothy 3:1). The words "perilous times"—*kairoi chalepoi* in Greek, can be translated as "times of stress." The cause, says Paul, is the behavior of people. Then he lists out 18 kinds of behavior that make for stress. The list in 3:2-5 reads like a description of our contemporary culture.

> Men will be lovers of themselves, lovers of money, boasters, proud, blasphemers, disobedient to parents, unthankful, unholy, unloving, unforgiving, slanderers, without self-control, brutal, despisers of good, traitors, headstrong, haughty, lovers of pleasure rather than lovers of God, having a form of godliness but denying its power.

Behavioral Consistency

Paul was deeply concerned in all his epistles, not only with doctrinal purity, but with behavioral consistency between belief and action, convictions and character, piety and personality. Throughout his epistles, and here in 2 Timothy, he persistently and decisively deals with the problem of people who name Christ as Lord but have not allowed Him to transform their personalities and character disorders.

None of us could read Paul's list of un-Christlike behavior without finding himself or herself in at least one of them in any one day. Sometimes several of them most every day. The list is a bracing inventory of the danger of apostate behavior in all of us.

The Form of Godliness, but Without Power

The last line, "having a form of godliness but denying its power," means believers who have the outward accoutrements of rites, rituals, and rules of religion, but in areas of their lives have denied the Lord's transforming power. That includes about all of us to some extent. All 18 of the character and personality disorders Paul lists out are a denial of the power of the Lord to change lives.

As we move through the inventory Paul's list provides, I pray that you and I will have the honesty to see areas in which we need to change and be given the courage to ask the Lord to change what needs to be changed. When you come to a category that does not apply to you, praise the Lord that you are not troubled with that. But dare to be boldly courageous. Make "I will be absolutely honest with myself and the Lord" your motto in the areas that are a problem to you and quench the Holy Spirit's fire.

Worship of the Perpendicular Pronoun

The first character disorder in Paul's list is worship of the perpendicular pronoun: "I." The apostle called people with this problem "lovers of themselves." The Greek word is *phil-autoi,* lovers of self, the opposite of lovers of God, *philotheoi.* The root, *phil*—love—is crucial. The fundamental problem Paul focuses on is misdirected love. The love the Holy Spirit gives us and seeks to direct to Christ and the Father through us, is squandered on one's self in indulgent self-centeredness. The breakdown of the love-relationship with God is the cause of the breakdown of our relationships with one another. All of the disorders Paul lists out are a result. The self is meant to be the container and transmitter of the Holy Spirit, not the object of worship instead of God.

The Problem of Self-Centeredness

The basic problem is self-centeredness. This is a sin we often tolerate in ourselves and suffer stress from in others. Self-centeredness must be seen for what it is: apostasy, the departure from loving God to inordinate, obsessive, and eventually compulsive focus on ourselves: what we want, how others treat us, our rights, our feelings. It is the direct opposite of healthy Christ-esteem, loving ourselves as loved by Him. Self-centeredness turns us inward on the self as worthy of worship; Christ-esteem fills the self with love for

God; for ourselves as forgiven and saved by His grace; and then turns us outward to live sacrificially for others.

The problem of self-centeredness is difficult to deal with because it often disguises itself. Sometimes our expressions of care and concern are really a desire to ingratiate people to us, or to keep them in our control; the focus is still on ourselves. Self-centeredness often parades itself in causes, issues, and theoretical theology. It can produce bogus leaders of factions where issues of dispute sound so righteous. The sure test is whether we want to come across as great or are focused on producing greatness in the people around us. Self-centeredness can ruin marriages, debilitate friendships, disrupt churches, and wreak havoc in political parties.

Now it is not for me to tell you if self-centeredness is ever your problem, in any degree, but you can. And if you do, and ask for the Holy Spirit to redirect your worship away from self to the Lord, He will show you how self-centeredness diminishes His fire within and will help you change.

Lovers of Money

Next in Paul's list of fire-quenchers are lovers of money. The word he used was *philarguros,* a compound combination of love, *phil,* and *arguros,* silver. In the apostle's first letter to Timothy, he had warned, "for the love of money is a root of all kinds of evil, for which some have strayed from the faith in their greediness and pierced themselves through with many arrows" (1 Timothy 6:10). Note that it is not money in itself, but the *love* of money. And here's the rub: getting and keeping a *little* money can become as much an obsession as guarding and clutching great wealth.

Don't miss the fact that money can become an idol of those who are believers. Subtle syncretism, the worship of more than one God, so easily can take place. The fire of the Spirit can be quenched by a love of money, or the things it can buy.

> *The love of money...robs us of our freedom; it causes a fitful anxiety, clouds our vision, and distorts our values.*

A friend who previously was on fire for Christ confided, "I'm alarmed by two things. I'm not thrilled by prayer and worship anymore, but I am by expanding my stock portfolio. I'm not proud of this, but becoming wealthy really excites me. But the more I acquire, the more I want."

A woman remarked, "I don't care about money, I just want more of what it can buy! You know: cars, more clothes, expensive jewelry, another house, social recognition." This woman was a leader in her church, attended a weekly Bible study, and said she loved Jesus. But what really turned her on was getting more stuff.

The problem most of us face is worry over money, having enough, paying bills, educating children and grandchildren, saving for retirement, becoming financially secure. The question is: When is our worry an evidence that the fires of faith have gone down and our security in Christ has been replaced by a quest for the security of money?

Philarguria, the love of money, is a spiritual virus that attacks the thinking brain. It robs us of our freedom; it causes a fitful anxiety, clouds our vision, and distorts our values. It is a cause of inordinate stress, the agitation of the nervous system, and often physical illness.

Some time ago, I developed a series of probing questions to help diagnose the extent the Spirit's fire in us may be being quenched by *philarguria.*

- Do you ever worry over money…having enough and keeping what you have?

- Is bill-paying time a stressful time for you?

- What about income tax time? Ever disturbed by reading your autobiography in the year's expenses?

- Has money ever been a source of argument or misunderstanding between you and another person?

- Do you sometimes experience twinges of competition, or even envy, over what others earn, have inherited, or have been able to do because of money they have and you don't?

- Have you ever equated your value as a person with what you earn?

- Can you remember a time when you bought clothing or things to solve hurt feelings, setbacks, or disappointments?

- Do you ever get anxious about whether you've done enough to save and prepare for retirement?

And here's a clincher:

- Do you spend more time thinking about money in any one day than you spend in prayer?

If you said yes to one or more of these questions, you may be having more of an affair with money than you thought. And once more, it may be a greater threat to your freedom than you realized.

Again, it is not for me to tell you, but you can.

The Boasters and the Proud, The Insulters and the Obstinate

The next two spiritual fire-quenchers in Paul's list are boasting and pride. The Greek word for boaster, *alazōn*, means one who pretends to be more than he or she is, and tries to create the impression of having more than he or she has. Originally, it was used of a wandering quack who made exaggerated claims for his services or product.

A boaster is not happy with the person he is, and tries to create the impression of being someone better, more capable, and more talented than he or she really is. The boaster is basically insecure.

Boasting quenches the Holy Spirit's fire because it denies the miraculous character transplant He is seeking to perform in us by making us like Christ through the imputation of the fruit of the Spirit: love, joy, peace, patience, kindness, goodness, faithfulness, gentleness, and self-control.

So boasting stunts growth in Christ and keeps us from pointing away from ourselves to the One who is the source of our strength, and the miracle of the new person He is creating. The psalmist had it right: "In God we boast all day long, and praise Your name forever" (Psalm 44:8). Boasting in ourselves is denying that all we have and are, have attained and achieved is because of the Lord.

The Proud

Closely related to boasters are the fire-quenchers who are proud. The word is *hyperēphanos,* again a compound, but this time two words that mean "to show oneself above." Few things pour cold water on the Holy Spirit's fire in us more than arrogant pride. I describe a person with false pride as one who worships his own maker, himself.

The particular emphasis in the word Paul uses for proud puts an emphasis on comparisons. We can think of ourselves as better, more capable, even more religious, only by comparing ourselves to others, and then putting ourselves above them. The Lord has called us to put our focus on Him, not on other people. If we are to make comparisons, they should be between us and Him. There's no place for pride in that comparison! You and I were programmed for greatness by making Him our magnificent obsession.

I like to read 2 Corinthians 5:17 with personal emphasis by using first person-singular pronouns. First, here's how it reads in *The Living Bible:* "When someone becomes a Christian, he becomes a brand new person inside. He is not the same anymore. A new life has begun!" Now, here's how it can read as our personal affirmation: "When I became a Christian, I became a brand new person inside. I'm not the same anymore. A new life has begun!"

It is impossible to experience this delight if we are distracted by comparing ourselves to another person and seeking to appear better or superior.

Well, what do you think? Ever quench the Holy Spirit's fire by boasting or false pride? It's not for me to say, but you know.

The reason it is so important to quell the fire-quencher of boasting and pride is that they foster another extinguisher of the Spirit.

Blasphemers

Paul goes on to expose blasphemers. You may react to the use of that word for a believer. The Greek word is *blasphēmia*, which really means *to insult*. We insult God when we act like we don't need Him and we insult people when we demean their worth by neglect or offensive disdain. Whether we put down or put off a person with hurting actions and wounding words, really, we are negating that person's value to God. A snub is a dub with a wrong name-expendable. George Bernard Shaw said, "The worst sin toward our fellow-creatures is not to hate them, but to be indifferent to them."

Ever been insulted? Remember the pain. Tempted to insult someone? Remember how it felt.

Breakers of the Fifth Commandment

Paul presses on in his lists of kinds of people who have the form of religion but not the power by citing those who neglect the Fifth Commandment by being disobedient to parents. The commandment to honor father and mother may have gone out of style in some families in our day, but not out of crucial importance to the solidarity of the family. We all know people who are Christians who do not honor the debt of gratitude they owe to those who brought them into the world. Family conflict may have left a person with unresolved issues with parents, living or in heaven.

Some never felt the affirmation so needed to become a mature person. Others lacked the creative discipline that develops maturity. Still others may have rebelled against their parents and have bad memories of their family life. On the other hand, many have fond memories of their parents and seek to emulate them in raising their own children.

Whatever the case, honoring parents is to see them as people with strengths and weaknesses, and to obey them as they seek to impart their faith, values, and priorities.

Disobedience is a strong word in Paul's phrase, "disobedience to parents." In Greek, *apeitheia* means the condition of being unpersuadable, obstinate. When the fire of the Holy Spirit burns within us, we become the opposite of obstinate. We become willing to follow the best that our parents sought to instill in us, and become champions of the family as the source of stability in these stressful times.

A Fearsome Fivesome

Next in the list of fire-quenchers is a fearsome fivesome—the unthankful, unholy, unloving, unforgiving, and slanderers. When we study the Greek words for these five common ways of quenching the fire of the Holy Spirit, we are alarmed by how often we may have expressed them ourselves!

The *unthankful (acharistoi)* are those who find it difficult to acknowledge that all they have is a gift. They act as though they have achieved and acquired everything on their own strength. Thanksgiving is humility that binds us to God and others. As we noted earlier, few things extinguish the fire of the Holy Spirit in us more than lack of gratitude. The flame is fueled when we can say with Joyce Kilmer, "Thank God for everything, but also thank God for…God," and with Paul to the Philippians, "I thank my God in all my remembrance of you" (Philippians 1:3). John Henry Jowett said, "Every virtue divorced from thankfulness is maimed and limps along the road." When the fires of excitement and enthusiasm over life die down, it is time to start thanking God for every blessing we have, and to begin saying to the people of our lives, "Thanks for being you!"

The *unholy (anosioi)* are worse than the unthankful. More than ingratitude, they have lost a sense of the sacredness of life, as well as its fundamental decencies. Respect for people, marriage, the family, and the beauty of the world around them is neglected or blatantly rejected. An on-fire Christian is meant to be just the opposite in expressing reverence for God, other people, and life itself. When the fire burns low, we too can lose our genuine appreciation for the privilege of being alive and belonging to the Lord.

Closely related to the unholy are the *unloving (astorgoi)*. *Storgē* is the Greek word for family love; *astorgē* is the denial of human affection between parents and children. We all know people who were starved for warm affection during their growing years, and find it difficult to give and receive love now. Worst of all, some of the *astorgoi* are those who are so self-centered and selfish that even the bonds of family love can be strained or broken. All we have to do is think of people who have rejected or sued relatives or family members while at the same time professing belief in God.

Some of the most disturbing of the fire-quenchers are the *unforgiving (aspondoi)*. *Sponde* means truce or agreement; *aspondoi* means those who refuse to make peace with those with whom they have quarreled. The word *aspondoi* also can mean those who break truces or agreements they have made. Bitterness and harshness can result. Whatever keeps us from forgiving those who have harmed us will also keep us from being ablaze with the Holy Spirit.

The fifth category of this fivesome is the verbal expression of unforgiving, implacable judgment by the *slander-ers*. The English word disturbs us; the Greek word behind it alarms us. It is *diabolos,* the word for *devil.* There is a devilish destruction that takes place when words are used to demean another person's character. Slander also can be verbal assassination of a political opponent. There is enough of both kinds in our time to dull the sensitivity to this distortion of people's character by direct attack or behind-the-back slurs that blur the reputations of good names.

It happens all the time these days. We see it on televised sessions of nomination hearings in Congress. Sadly, we hear it in conflict in local churches and denominations, and we overhear it in gossip sessions among otherwise committed Christians. Words are cheap, and to use them to question another person's character is a cheap shot. A good rule is never to say anything about a person you have not said face-to-face—and said with a caring, constructive intent. That would silence a lot of slander.

Now allow me to reiterate: It is not for me to say whether you express any of the above fearsome fivesome, but you may want to take an incisive inventory that may lead to honest confession.

Losing Self-Control

Paul's list of spiritual fire-quenchers goes on. The next category is those without self-control *(akrateis)*. The Greek verb *kratein* means to control; *akrateis* are those who are without control. We all know from personal experience or observation of others around us, what a debilitating and discouraging thing it is to be out of self-control. We'd all like to be able to keep control of our emotions, our outbursts, our resentments, our appetites, our thought-life.

Self-control is the result of Spirit-control. Moment-by-moment, hour after hour, day in and day out, we need to trust to the Holy Spirit the control of our wills. When we *admit* that we tend to lose control in an area, *submit* to the Holy Spirit's control, and *commit* to Him our compulsive, often addictive behavior, He can and does give us supernatural strength.

We dare not mock the sometime slow, difficult process of yielding to the Holy Spirit's control. At the same time, we should refrain from glib shibboleths like, "Get control of yourself!" to ourselves, loved ones, and friends. The specific prayer, "Holy Spirit, strengthen my will, take control," is the secret of gaining creative self-control.

Is there any aspect of your life that needs Holy Spirit–inspired self-control? It is not for me to tell you, but you can. If you do, the Holy Spirit will give you power. Try Him!

You Talking to Me?

The next group of fire-quenchers in Paul's list of people who have the form of godliness but deny its power at first doesn't seem to apply to people like you and me. Pretty strong terms for the likes of you and me. Brutal, despisers of good, traitors, headstrong, haughty? But look again.

Ever been brutal in a lack of sensitiveness or sympathy? Ever write off a person or say, "If I never see that person again it will be too soon"?

"Despisers of good" may not be an adequate translation of *aphilagathoi*, one who has no love for the good. But how would one who has no passion to strive for what is God's good get that way? Little by little, one compromise after another, resistant to the Spirit's inspiration, we can tire of working for what's good. A bland neutrality sets in. Where are you, where am I, in the never-ending battle for excellence in everything we do and say?

When I mention traitors, you may want to say, "Wait a minute, I'm willing to own up to a lot, but I'm no traitor!" Paul's use of this word must be seen in the light of the conditions of the time he wrote this last letter to Timothy. Christianity had been outlawed in the Roman Empire.

> *It is difficult to be inspired by the Holy Spirit when we are inflated by self-aggrandizement.*

Informing the Roman government about believers had become a frightening danger. Sometimes those who were within the church betrayed their fellow believers out of personal envy or a struggle for control.

Today we are forced to question whether loyalty to fellow Christians sometimes is not destroyed by our differences in denominations, political views, and controversial issues. We betray Christ when we are traitors to the cause of unity. Remember that the conservative and liberal wings come from the same bird!

Headstrong? The Greek word is *propeteis,* meaning precipitous, impulsive, and imperious. A headstrong person thinks he is always right, wants what he wants when he wants it, and is insensitive to what others think or need. He doesn't listen. Why should he? He has a corner on all truth! This spiritual proclivity makes relationships difficult and fellowship impossible.

The haughty are not just headstrong, they are swell-headed. It is difficult to be inspired by the Holy Spirit when we are inflated by self-aggrandizement. And yet, we've all known times when we've wanted recognition, were hurt when we were slighted or overlooked, or manipulated to be sure we were applauded.

Known by What We Love

Paul concludes the list of fire-quenchers by reminding us that we will be known by what we love. The last category is lovers of pleasure rather than lovers of God. Before we dismiss that proclivity as having no application to us, stop for a moment and ask, "By my own admission, in conversation with friends, people at work, and acquaintances in the community, what would they say is the love of my life?"

What is the pleasure that excites us and thrills us? Would anyone say, "Now there's a person who really loves God!"? One sure way of showing that would be the way we love our families. The salient point is that the Holy Spirit wants to set us ablaze with love for the Father, Christ, and the people in our lives. Putting anything ahead of these priorities will quench His fire. With His fire, all of life can be a pleasure!

. . . .

We have considered each one of the 18 manifestations of self-centeredness among believers, as well as unbelievers in the world. My prayer is that this inventory will be a source of self-examination and an exposure to any of the fire-quenchers that may be dousing the fire of the Spirit in you. Put directly: Are you and I acting like any of these?

In faithfulness to Paul's description of people who have the form of godliness but not the power, what do we do with His incisive statement, "And from such people turn away!" As we stated earlier, Paul is concerned about the purity of the church, both doctrinally and behaviorally. The church is meant to be a hospital for redeemed sinners who are being healed and set free. It was not, however, intended to be a collecting place of religious sinners who continually resist the power of the Holy Spirit to change them. Un-Christlike behavior must be confronted in ourselves and others, exposed to the Spirit's healing power, and transformed. The behavioral standards of followers of Christ and what is totally unacceptable behavior for believers must be taught, preached, discussed in small groups and in conversation.

The "Well, that's just the way he is!" and "She's always been that way!" accommodation of self-centeredness is not love, but toleration of behavior and character that will quench the fire of the Holy Spirit.

. . . .

CHAPTER SEVEN

Leaping Flames
of Resiliency

*I wish there were some wonderful place
In the Land of Beginning Again:
Where all our mistakes and all our heartaches
And all our poor selfish greed
Could be dropped like a shabby old coat at the door
And never put on again.*[9]

The Land of Beginning Again is home territory for those who have the fire of the Holy Spirit burning on the hearth of their hearts. The flame leaps up with resiliency.

Resiliency is the bounce-back blessing. The actual meaning of resiliency is to return to a previous condition. It also means being capable of withstanding shock without permanent deformation or rupture; tending to regain strength or high spirits after weakness or depression; the ability to make a fresh start.

Extending the metaphor of the red ember in the white ash, resiliency is the sure outward sign of someone who consistently receives the fresh burst of the Lord's billows. The fire of the Holy Spirit within us can fuel this remarkable quality of bouncing back after discouragements, disappointments, difficulties, and defeats. We may get knocked down by life, but we are never knocked out!

Bounce-Back Vitality

We all face times when we need the bounce-back vitality of Holy Spirit-inspired resiliency. We may not have been called to recover from excruciating circumstances, but you and I go through blows to our esteem, depleting criticism, failures, defeats, setbacks, reversals, bouts with depression, and problems with people that disturb and distress us. Life has its tough times, when only the Holy Spirit can give us the courage to begin again. Trouble is a stranger to none of us. The question is not whether we've had testing times, but how we have recovered from them.

For over 50 years, I've cared for people as a pastor. It is amazing how some survive the blows of life and bounce back, while others lack the energizing power of a resilient spirit. I've also talked to leaders through the years. One of the things they long for in themselves and look for in those they want to hire and entrust with heavy responsibility is this wonderful gift of resiliency.

The Resilient Paul

One of the best examples of resiliency in the Spirit is the apostle Paul. Talk about the bounce-back blessing! Paul faced every kind of problem and perplexity. His last will and testament—2 Timothy—is really a survival kit on resiliency. We are given an opportunity to listen in on his personal reaffirmation of the qualities that are woven into the uplifting cord of true resiliency. The apostle does not admonish Timothy to try harder to acquire these qualities, but instead, commends the way Timothy has sought to emulate them. Good teaching! He recruited Timothy to be on Timothy's own team in facing tough times. Second Timothy 3:10-11 is a wonderful description of spiritual resiliency set in contrast to the stressmongers we discussed in the previous chapter. Paul says to Timothy,

> You have carefully followed my doctrine, manner of life, purpose, faith, longsuffering, love, perseverance, persecutions, afflictions, which happened to me...

Thinking Clearly

The first thing Paul commended Timothy for following in his example was his doctrine. The word is *didaskalia,* teaching. Resiliency in life's ups and downs is not dependant on how we feel, but what we think. Feelings follow thought.

Paul's resiliency was the result of carefully thought-out convictions. He could bounce back in tough times because he believed that, in spite of difficulties, the Father is sovereign of all, Christ is with us as Lord of all, and the Holy Spirit is the indwelling source of strength to endure and conquer over all.

From these reasoned convictions come the powerful presuppositions that give us resiliency in crises. God does not send suffering, cause tragedies, or try us with difficulties. We can dismiss the false question so often asked in natural disasters or humanly caused problems, "Where was God when this happened?" Our conviction is that He is with us, giving us courage and hope.

We believe that God created humankind to know, love, and serve Him. We reverently reflect on what must have been His most crucial decision: to allow us to live in a fallen world, giving us freedom of will, knowing that there can be no response of love to Him without choice, but also knowing that we might abuse and misuse our freedom.

Also, we know that there is an objective force of evil in the world that often is expressed through people, movements, and nations. Heinous acts happen. God is not dissuaded. He shares the suffering of those who are victims of evil, and in ways we could not imagine, brings good in spite of evil. When we trust Him in tough times, He gives us courage.

. . . .

Our sure foundation in trying times is that God sent Christ into the world to incarnate His love. Christ died on the cross as the once, never to be repeated, substitutionary sacrifice for our sins and our reconciliation to the Father. Christ confronted and defeated the power of death and vanquished Satan's influence over those who trust in Him as Lord and Savior. Now, on this side of Calvary, an open tomb and Pentecost, we have an assurance that this life is but a small part of eternity. In the midst of anguish or grief over the death of loved ones, we are reminded that death is not an ending for those who believe in Christ, but a transition in living. We bounce back from discouragement with resiliency. All because of the clear conviction that "though the wrong seems oft so strong, God is the ruler yet!"

In my experience counseling people who have gone through trouble of all kinds, I have learned that those who, prior to crises, have done the hard thinking under the guidance of the Holy Spirit, are able to endure and rise above their misfortune, physical suffering, or mental stress.

During 9/11, its aftermath, and the anthrax crisis in Washington, I witnessed firsthand the strength and confidence of those who had firm convictions, and also the panic that gripped those who had never thought through the tough questions. It was a time to think clearly about God's sovereignty over America and His plan for our nation in the family of nations. In prayer meetings, Bible studies, and a special session of senators and members of the House of Representatives in the Capitol rotunda, we reaffirmed that the only lasting, long-range antidote to terrorism is righteousness as a nation. We cannot cease to be the nation we were destined to be by losing the very quality that caused the terrorists to attack us.

Patriotism has not gone out of style. Following 9/11, it was wonderful to sense the resiliency of leaders and staff as a result of basic convictions about God's sovereignty over our nation all through our history.

The Secret of Greatness

Belief in the sovereignty of God provides a sense of destiny. He rules over all and calls men and women to be servant leaders under His control. William Blake said, "Great things happen when men and mountains meet; the rest go jostling in the street." The founders of our nation firmly believed they were called by God to establish this new nation.

Further, belief in the sovereignty of God provides supernatural power. "The LORD your God is God of gods and Lord of lords, the great God, mighty and awesome" (Deuteronomy 10:17). There is supernatural power available for supernatural leadership. The gifts of wisdom beyond human understanding, knowledge beyond education, vision beyond our grandest imagination are given to those who surrender control over their lives and their leadership to the Lord's control.

Finally, belief in the sovereignty of God produces indomitable courage.

> *God moves in a mysterious way*
> *His wonders to perform;*
> *He plants His footsteps in the sea*
> *And rides upon the storm.*
>
> *Deep in unfathomable mines*
> *Of never failing skill*
> *He treasures up His bright designs*
> *And works His sovereign will.*[10]

I have a Scots friend who ends conversations in which we have shared our challenges by saying, "Take courage, lad—it's yours, you know!" His bracing admonition is in keeping with Jesus' inspiring imperative, "In the world you have tribulation, but take courage; I have overcome the world" (John 16:33). Courage is the "can dare to do" impetus of the bounce-back blessing of authentic resiliency. Take it; it's yours!

Make a personal inventory: In times of crisis in your own personal life, what are the irrevocable, irreducible convictions to which you can turn? When you sink through the shifting sands of difficulties, what basic beliefs about God and His reliability become the rock of ages on which you can stand?

Conduct Follows Convictions

The second quality Paul affirmed that Timothy was emulating in being a resilient person was his "manner of life." The Greek word Paul used was *agōgē*, meaning conduct or discipline, the way or course of life. For Paul, prayer was the secret of living out his convictions.

In prayer, we can admit our need, submit our problems, demit our own control, and commit our future to the Lord. When we follow these steps of prayer, the Lord shows us where we may be wrong, or gives us courage to hold fast if He affirms we are right.

Recently, I had a disturbing disagreement with a friend. It ended in a truce, but no reconciliation. I didn't sleep much the following night. About four in the morning, I followed the admit, submit, demit, and commit steps of prayer. To my astonishment, the Lord showed me I was wrong in my attitude. When I admitted my part in the misunderstanding, immediately I was able to commit to sharing that with my friend. Not only that, I had to change my attitude and behavior.

I've had just the opposite result in other situations. When I admit, submit, demit, and commit, often I'm confirmed in my position or actions, and hear the Lord whisper, "Stay the course, you are right."

In either case, resiliency happens when I give up my control and surrender to the Lord's control.

Intimate prayer is the mightiest force in the world. If God knows, why pray? So often, God waits to help us solve problems until we pray. He wants to use the need to draw us closer to Him. We do not pray to change the mind of God, but to receive it. Prayer is the native tongue of the Land of Beginning Again!

The Power of Purpose and the Gift of Faith

The next secret of resiliency that Paul commends in Timothy is purpose. The Greek word is *prothesei*, meaning a setting forth, a statement. Paul knew who he was because he knew Whose he was. His purpose was clear: to live for Christ, to preach Christ, and to win others to believe in Christ. He called Timothy back to this same purpose.

Recently, my life became burdened with an overloaded schedule of travel and speaking, along with a lot of other demands. The question was, what does God want me to do with the rest of my life? I had to reestablish priorities around my purpose to be a communicator of grace. Time in prayer and Bible study was ranked first. Quality time with my wife and family came next. Exercise, recreation, and relaxation came next. Then, out of all the good opportunities I had in my professional life, preaching, writing, and teaching came next in my priority list. When I had finished my list, I felt fresh courage to say "no" to things weighing on me, and "yes" to things that were clearly guided. Resiliency returned. I bounced back to enjoy living again.

A Resilient Faith

Press on with Paul as he commends Timothy for receiving the gift of faith. For the apostle, there were two kinds of faith: primary faith to accept our salvation, and pertinacious faith to claim those special blessings the Lord has prepared. One level of faith assures us that we will live forever, the other enables us to live abundantly during the years of this portion of our eternal life. When we prayerfully seek to know what the Lord desires, often we are shown a possibility which is beyond achieving on our own strength. The key is to believe that the Lord provides for what He guides. He will open closed doors, provide willing helpers, smooth out the rough places in the road ahead when we are willing to pray for His will and then pray for the boldness to attempt it with His supernatural intervention to help us pull it off.

What does this wonder-working quality of faith have to do with resiliency? Everything. We bounce back after life's difficulties with a vision that the Lord is able and will grant us strength to move on in life. It's the exciting sense of expectation of what He will do that produces the lively burst of resiliency. We send up a cheer in the Land of Beginning Again.

Bouncing Back After Being Hurt

The next three strands of the cord of true resiliency help us to endure with patience. Paul affirms Timothy's effort to respond to life with "longsuffering, love, and perseverance." I like to think of the first and third being an expression of the second. It is divine love

> *We bounce back repeatedly when we are sure that what we are enduring is being used for His glory.*

flowing through us that enables us to keep on loving in spite of what people or groups do to hurt us.

The first kind of love-motivated patience Paul emphasizes is *makrothumia,* a quality of *patience expressed for people.* What people say and do *can* hurt us deeply. People do what they do because of who they really are inside, and can change what they do only as the Lord changes them inside. When we become upset with people, there is no bounce-back until we surrender them to the Lord and thank Him in advance for whatever change He intends to make in them. We become resilient when we let go of recrimination, our assumed right to punish with our actions or attitudes. "Judgment is mine" says the Lord.

The second kind of love-motivated patience Paul affirms in Timothy is *hupomone* in Greek. This word is a compound of *hupo*—under, and *menō*—to abide. With the fires of love burning in the hearth of our hearts, we are given the *ability to remain under difficult circumstances.* This kind of patience produces long-pull faithfulness in trying circumstances. We can't attempt it unless we do it for love and by love.

The crucial issue is to be sure that staying in circumstances that demand this kind of patience has been guided by the Lord. It is perilous to doggedly persist in circumstances even though the Lord has not communicated His call to stay there. Conversely, it is a joy to receive supernatural strength to stay put where the Lord has placed us. We bounce back repeatedly when we are sure that what we are enduring is being used for His glory.

◥ ◣ ◢

Paul reminds Timothy of specific circumstances in which the apostle exemplified bounce-back resiliency. It is significant that he adds Lystra to the places where he suffered. That was Timothy's hometown. During the first missionary journey, Timothy's mother and grandmother were converted to Christ. It was also the place where Paul was stoned and left for dead. I have often imagined that young Timothy saw the apostle rise up and walk out of the stoning pit. Resiliency indeed! No wonder that when Paul returned on his second missionary journey, Timothy was ready to join him as he moved on to preach Christ throughout the then-known world.

We all need heroes and heroines who have shown us authentic resiliency. Also, with humility and praise to the Lord, we need to remember those times when He surprised us with strength to bounce back after painful blows to self-esteem, or health, or plans for the future. Thinking about those times prepares us for a new burst of resiliency. But by far the most important secret to nonstop resiliency is to claim our citizenship in that wonderful Land of Beginning Again.

Now, before you turn the page to begin the next chapter, think of the relationships and circumstances in which you need the bounce-back blessing. The Lord is more ready to give it than you may be to ask. "If anyone is in Christ, he is a new creation; old things have passed away; behold, all things have become new" (2 Corinthians 5:17). And I say all things keep on becoming new when the fire within us keeps leaping up with resiliency.

CHAPTER EIGHT

Kindling a Goal for Today Big Enough for Eternity

he cartoon caught my attention.

A dignified-looking man was on his knees, praying. His head was raised up, looking to heaven. There was an insistent, imploring expression on his face. At the bottom of the cartoon were the words of his prayer: "In the name of the Freedom of Information Act, I demand to know what's in my file!"

We laugh with empathy and identification. We hear a lot about the files kept on us about everything from credit ratings to taxes. Also, every so often we think about our goals for our lives and wonder how we're doing in accomplishing our purpose. Ever think about your eternal file? Ever wonder about whether you are accomplishing the reason you were born? Do you have a goal for today that's big enough for eternity? "Lord, am I reaching Your goal for me? What's in my file?"

Daily Progress in Our Eternal Goal

We all are in the process of progressing to or resisting progress toward what we envision is the ultimate goal of our lives. Once we have established our long-range goal for our lives, we can do a daily accountability check. That way we can make progress toward our purpose.

Also, if our goal is grand enough, we are able to take in stride the difficulties or delights of life and discern how they have brought us closer to our vision. Is our goal for living today big enough to express our ultimate goal?

A loved one dies, a close friend faces a life-threatening disease, a neighbor who seemed healthy is told that his days are numbered. Suddenly, we feel uneasy. We wonder, "What if this were my last day? Would the accumulation of all my days equal the achievement of my life goal?"

At the end of his life, the apostle Paul could look back and see how his goal had strengthened and sustained him. What he wrote Timothy in retrospect about what he had accomplished, I really think was a statement of what had been his goal all through his Christian life. "I have fought the good fight, I have finished the race, I have kept the faith" (2 Timothy 4:7).

. . . .

Paul's retrospective reflection provides us with a perspective resolve in defining our goal for today that's big enough for eternity. The apostle became the intentional person he was because his goal had been set before he began his adventuresome all-stops-out life in Christ. His goal to fight the good fight, run the race, and keep the faith was a three-part expression of Paul's passion: "To me, to live is Christ" (Philippians 1:21).

The Good Fight

The first part of the goal for today big enough for eternity is to fight the good fight. The Greek word Paul used for fight is *agōna*. It means a contest in the athletic arena. The word for good is *kalon,* that which is intrinsically good and accomplishes its purpose. A good athletic contest is one in which an athlete performs to the best of his ability, to the full extent of his strength and skill, and with every fiber and facet of his being. When we say an athlete has given his all, he has fought a good fight. He is intentional.

Paul could look back over the 30 years of his ministry since his conversion and say that every day he had held nothing back. The Lord had all of Paul there was.

A wonderful way to live! To fight the good fight each day is to live that day as if it were our last. A lifetime of days like that adds up to a truly great life. In the contest of life, we battle with mediocrity, laziness, or self-indulgence.

Until we win the battle within, we can't do battle with the opponents that confront us in the world around us. With help from the Holy Spirit, we can persist in the battle with discouragement, doubt, and depression.

After Paul's time of preparation for his ministry, he was ready to do battle with legalism and justification by works in Judaism, with false gods and pagan rituals in the religions of his time, and with social injustice and unrighteousness. Day by day, traveling the then-known world, he talked, preached, and debated in the battle for the truth.

In the same way, we confront the social issues of poverty, racism, prejudice, and inequality. Also, we are called to stand fast in our commitment to communicate the gospel to those who don't know Christ.

Finishing the Race

Paul uses another athletic image when he affirms that he has finished the race. Every day of the apostle's life, his goal had been to finish a lap in the race to know, love, and serve Christ. Now at the end of his life, he could say that he had finished the race. His daily goal was big enough for eternity. He had forcefully stated that goal throughout his life.

"One thing I do," Paul wrote the Philippians, "forgetting those things which are behind and reaching forward to those things which are ahead, I press toward the goal for the prize of the upward call of God in Christ Jesus" (Philippians 3:13-14).

It is fascinating to note that in the Greek there is no word for "do." It should read, "One thing…forgetting those things which are behind…" One thing indeed. One passion, one purpose, one plan. Christ!

Our goal is to *press* toward the goal. The descriptive Greek word, *epekteinomenos* is used, meaning "stretching forward, out toward the goal line." That means to run flat out, with arms outstretched to reach the goal. Again, the note of energetic intentionality. The Greek word for prize is *brabeion*, from the word that means umpire, or the one who awards the prize. Again, for us it is Christ Himself. And the "upward call"? Graduation to heaven!

Eric Liddell, of *Chariots of Fire* fame, said, "When I run fast, I feel I give God pleasure." And so can we in the race of life. Today and forever.

Keeping the Faith

Further, Paul affirmed that he had kept the faith. Again, the note was a positive, enthusiastic, all-out intentionality. Reflecting on Paul's life, we can see that keeping the faith was his constantly-repeated mission statement.

Remember the twofold commitment we talked about in chapter 2. Paul knew the Lord in whom he had believed and was persuaded that the Lord would keep what he had committed to Him. Then the Apostle reminded Timothy to keep what had been committed to him. *Phulassō*, to guard, watch over, keep safe, is used. Now, in this concluding passage, 2 Timothy 4:7, the word is *tetereka,* perfect, active, indicative of *tereō,* indicating a strong, determined effort to keep the faith. Paul may have meant that he had kept faith with Christ. More likely, "the faith" was the gospel, the composite of the basic ingredients of the Lordship of Christ, justification by faith in Him alone, the atonement of Calvary, the resurrection of Christ, and His reigning power over history. Paul had never deserted Christ, nor the salvation that was offered in Him alone.

Paul had kept the faith, because the Lord had kept him safe until the end. The apostle never gave up on Christ because Christ held him in His care, never giving up on him.

Dr. Alexander Whyte, a famous preacher at St. George's West in Edinburgh, Scotland, in another generation, was walking down Princess Street when a member of his congregation called out to him a colloquial vernacular greeting, "Dr. Whyte, how are you keeping?" The great preacher paused and answered, "I'm not keeping a'tall; I'm being kept!"

Keeping the faith is a vital part of our primary goal that's big enough for eternity. In fact, faith in Christ as Lord and Savior is the basic qualification for graduating into heaven. Day by day, we affirm that Christ is our eternal security, our ever-present strength, and our never-failing source of courage and hope. We can live each day without reservation or reserve, tackling each challenge with gusto. Keeping the faith is also keeping faith with Christ, seeking to be faithful to Him. Paul encouraged the Colossian Christians to adopt the motto: "Whatever you do in word or deed, do all in the name of the Lord Jesus, giving thanks to God the Father through Him" (Colossians 3:17).

Before you read on, pause to reflect on what has been your goal in living each day of your life. Is it a goal big enough for eternity? Does it give you confidence?

The Crown of Righteousness

Paul's confidence was vibrant: "Finally, there is laid up for me the crown of righteousness" (2 Timothy 4:8). The apostle had claimed his righteousness through Christ every day. The crown of righteousness laid up for him in heaven was to be a triumphant recognition of his justification by faith in Christ alone. It would be a recognition of his accomplished goal to live life to the fullest, giving his all, flat-out reaching for the goal line, and living out his trust in Christ in every circumstance. Just as an athlete in the Greek games was given a crown of victory at the end of a race, so too Paul's crown was waiting for him.

An Exciting Assurance

Don't miss the exciting assurance this gives us. In a way, we are running a race with the confidence that we have won already. Note that Paul was convinced that the crown had already been laid up for him. The same is true for us. We are right with God through faith in Christ. Our destiny was settled the day we believed. Remember, it was not our doing, but a gift through the influence and inspiration of the Holy Spirit. Faith was a gift, and so was the status we were given. So it is not the good works we have done or will do, but our righteousness through Christ that lays up for us the crown of righteousness. We are not working our way to heaven by our goodness. Our crown is not being forged by each good deed we do. It is already laid up for us.

Amazing thing. The knowledge of our eternal security spurs us on to live without strain or stress and serve the Lord with joy and delight. The very thing some people do to try to earn their way to heaven, we do enthusiastically because we are sure we're going there!

The Righteous Judge

The one whom Paul was sure would give him the crown of righteousness was Christ, the righteous judge. The title of judge for Christ is a further source of confidence for our daily living. We meet Christ as our judge each day. He helps us define our goal big enough for eternity, and judges the extent to which we live in keeping with that goal each day.

Passing with Flying Colors

Christ wants us to pass our eternal examination with flying colors. Through the Holy Spirit, He preps us for our final examination.

I remember the very different approaches to final exams three of my professors took when I was in postgraduate school. One always included a trick question in the final exam. However much you studied, you could not be prepared for that question.

Another professor was just the opposite. He didn't require a final exam at all. "What grade do you think you deserve?" he would ask. Finishing his course was like appearing in a courtroom without a judge. There was no accountability.

> *The fires of passion the Spirit has fueled will have motivated us to love sacrificially, serve others creatively, and face difficulties triumphantly*

A third professor was most helpful. He would give us students all the questions that would be on the examination at the end of the semester. If we studied hard, and knew the answers to those questions, we'd pass with a top grade. In the process of getting ready for the exam, we realized that the questions covered all the key material in the course. The professor wanted to be sure that we passed having learned all that he had tried to teach us.

In a similar, but vastly more crucial way, the Holy Spirit wants us to know the questions that we'll be asked each day, and on our last day. It is His assignment to be sure we'll pass right on through to glory. His gift of faith enables us to declare Christ as our Savior and Lord. The fires of passion the Spirit has fueled will have motivated us to love sacrificially, serve others creatively, and face difficulties triumphantly.

Note that Paul assures Timothy that the crown of righteousness is waiting for those who have loved Christ's appearing. A goal for today that is big enough for eternity is to love the Lord's incarnate appearance in history, 2000 years ago, the way He continues to appear in response to our daily prayer today, and in the way He will appear at the end of history. When we have fully appreciated all that Christ did at His first coming, we become expectant of His interventions into our lives today, and eager for His second coming.

Now, back to where we started this chapter, with the man in the cartoon. We can be sure what's in our eternal file. Records of all of the sins, failures, and mistakes have been re-moved because of Calvary. They will not be used against us. There will be a record of our belief in Christ as Savior and Lord, and the list of times we cared for the needs of people as if serving Christ Himself. And, since Christ has called us to live with intentionality, I think there will be honorable men-tions of the fact that the fire of our passion for living was kindled by daily renewal of our goal that was big enough for eternity.

James Hudson Taylor said, "Do not have your concert first and tune your instruments later." I would agree. Later may be too late!

CHAPTER NINE

Fanning the Fellowship of the Flaming Heart

◼ ◼ ◼

We can't go at it alone. We need what John Calvin called the fellowship of the flaming heart.

In the concluding verses of Paul's very personal second letter to Timothy, he indirectly shows the way the eternal flame can be fueled and fanned by others and ways it can be stifled and smothered by them. The last section of Paul's letter is both autobiographical about his own needs and biographical about the lives of friends, some of whom have delighted him, and others who have disappointed him.

◼ ◼ ◼

I'm very moved by Paul's honesty. He is open and vulnerable about his own physical and emotional needs in those last days in prison. He admits his loneliness, and longs for Timothy to come before winter sets in and a sea voyage would be impossible. The apostle asks Timothy to bring along a cloak he had left with a man named Carpus at Troas, and not to forget his books, and especially his parchments. He does not pretend he can make it alone; he needs his friends. The "fellowship of the flaming heart" was essential to tending the eternal flame.

Affectionately, Paul affirmed that Luke, the beloved physician, was with him (4:11). They had traveled together and spread the Gospel ever since Paul had a vision of him in a dream during his time in Troas and sailed over to Macedonia. I've always thought that Luke was the man of Macedonia who appeared in Paul's dream saying, "Come over to Macedonia and help us" (Acts 16:9). It is after this that the "we" passages of Acts, which was written later by Luke, begin. From that point on, Luke and Paul were inseparable. Luke ministered to the apostle's physical needs and provided sustaining companionship.

No Solo Flights

We were never meant to make it alone. There are no solo flights in dynamic discipleship. Honestly admitting our need for others is a salient secret for keeping the fire of the Holy Spirit aglow within us.

As I think back over the years, I realize the Lord has never allowed me to try to keep the flame burning alone.

As I mentioned earlier, I began the Christian life in my freshman year in college in the fellowship of caring friends whose faith was contagious. Both Bruce Larson and Ralph Osborne, who introduced me to Christ, became part of my first experience of the fellowship of the flaming heart. They have been among my closest friends for 55 years. Over these years, we've shared mountaintops and valleys of life. We've been through grief and pain, as well as inexpressible triumphs and victories.

Together we discovered the power of the honest, open life. We've shared our failures and successes, our concerns and our convictions. When we ask each other the familiar question "How are you?" it is always an invitation to share our souls, what is on our minds, and what may be troubling us. Because of these two brothers, all through my personal and professional life, I've always had the benchmark of what the fellowship of the flaming heart was meant to be.

Wherever the Lord has moved me, He has provided me with a new group of fellow adventurers in the Spirit: seminary; postgraduate school in Scotland; my first parish in Winnetka, Illinois; then ten years in Bethlehem, Pennsylvania; then twenty-three years in Hollywood, California; then on to eight years as Chaplain of the United States Senate; and now writing, teaching, and traveling the length and breadth of the nation speaking.

In each period, I've had the great advantage of an accountability group. The fire of the Holy Spirit and my prayer partners constantly re-ignited, billowed, and refueled the fire in me.

In the United States Senate, in addition to the Bible studies I taught, my own spiritual fire was fanned by a small group of senators with whom I met consistently. Each of us had an opportunity to share each week where he was in his spiritual pilgrimage, and then receive support, encouragement, and empowering prayer. The following week, we would report back on progress or continued problems. We all learned to take no one for granted. Power, position, and prestige might be polished on the surface, but inside we all had needs. Honest vulnerability made it possible for us to care for each other. We tended the flame in each other.

Today, the adventure continues in my present challenges and opportunities. Brothers in Christ like Dr. Jack Hayford and Bishop Ken Ulmer provide accountability and encouragement. We've been through a lot together in Los Angeles: the Shepherds' Love L.A. movement of pastors, the riots, crises in ministry, awesome expansion of our individual ministries, tri-chairing of the Billy Graham crusade, and pressing on each other in the pursuit of excellence. We laugh and cry, share and pray. It is a delight to be a part of a group of brothers who seek to be to each other what Christ has been to each of us.

Those positive experiences help me to feel what Paul's friends meant to him. They also enable me to sense the excruciating disappointment he felt with those who did not stay in fellowship, and drifted away. The flame in them burned low, and could no longer be fanned by the fellowship.

The One Who Drifted Away

Demas, who defected from the fellowship, is an example of what can happen to the fires within us when we drift away from our primary commitment to Christ and dependence on the Holy Spirit. I call it the Demas drift. Paul writes with a deep pathos and profound concern for Demas: "Demas has forsaken me, having loved this present world, and has departed for Thessalonica" (4:10).

The New Testament is very straightforward about the drama of the early church. It exposes the weaknesses as well as the strengths of our heroines and heroes of the faith. It also tells us about some who didn't make it. People who had a glorious beginning and a tragic end. Demas was one of those. We know very little about him, except what Paul tells us in three different references.

During his first imprisonment in Rome, Paul wrote to Philemon and referred to Demas in verse 24: "Mark, Aristarchus, Demas, Luke, my fellow laborers." That's quite a Hall of Fame in which to be included. Then, in Colossians 4:14, the apostle's enthusiasm obviously has dampened. Demas is mentioned, but without commendation or affirmation. "Luke the beloved physician and Demas greet you." Then, in the 2 Timothy passage we are considering, Paul is very forthright about being forsaken by Demas because he "loved this present world, and has departed for Thessalonica."

What happened? Why would the apostle Paul depict Demas with faint praise, and then state so forcefully his defection and departure? What did Paul observe in Demas that would reflect the apostle's change in attitude?

Bishop Handley C.G. Moule, in his devotional commentary on 2 Timothy, said that he could not read this account on Demas without misty eyes. I would empathize. I think of people who have drifted from accountability to the fellowship of the flaming heart, and whose fires have burned low.

Paul gives us a clue to what happened to Demas. "Having loved this present world, and...departed for Thessalonica" tells us a great deal. If we were to make a graph of the life of Demas, and put the full abundant life in Christ on one side, and on the other, defection and defeat, the line on the graph would chart a glorious beginning and a sad ending.

The Spirit of the Age

When did this happen? Dig deeper into the text. The answer is there. The word for "world" in the Greek text is not *kosmos,* but *aiōn,* the age. The word "age" was used not only for a period of time, but for the economic, intellectual, and philosophical ethos of a particular span of years. There was a spirit of an age.

Demas forsook Paul and the fellowship because he was in love with the spirit of the age. Over a period of time, his commitment to Christ was crowded out by an ever-encroaching involvement in, and eventually, surrender to, the ethos and spirit of that age. We contrast that with what Paul wrote to Timothy in his first epistle: "Fight the good fight... lay hold on eternal life" (1 Timothy 6:12). The same basic root is in the words "eternal life." *Aiōniou*—"eternal" in the Greek—really means "of the ages." It is the descriptive word that identifies not one age, but all the ages. Eternal life is continuous, unending ages.

In Christ, we have an ageless life, one not limited to the age in which we are living. Demas loved the age, the ethos, of his present life. He was enamored by and committed to the diminutive gods of Roman power and culture.

It can happen to any of us. There is an ethos to the age in which we are living. It is comprised of materialism, secularism, competition, and relativism. It is possible to become so dependant on our age that Christ is crowded out. Authority, titles, success, all the accoutrements of success in material wealth and possessions can become our source of security. It is easy to pick up the lingo, jargon, values, techniques, and standards of our present age.

The same can happen to a church. It can become so reflective of culture that it lacks a bracing word for the culture. The result is that people are not called to question the false gods of the age and experience the lasting peace of an ageless assurance. The syncretism of "Jesus plus" the values of culture begins the Demas drift. It doesn't happen all at once; it is subtle, seductive. We can express our faith in church, but inside we are sold out to culture. The zest is gone.

The alternative is to make Christ and our ageless, eternal life, of the ages, the driving passion of our lives. Then we can live with freedom and joy in this age, without selling our souls to it. The accolade of our Lord is more important than the accumulation of our private kingdom of thingdom. Perspective is everything. Who is our Lord? This age or Christ?

The signs of the Demas drift are when we have less time for prayer and when we get focused on our own image, popularity, and success. Are we closer to Christ than last year, last month, last week? Is our relationship with Him more vital, committed, empowered, and exciting than ever before? And what about our impact on this present age? Are we involved in serving people and giving ourselves and our money to relieve suffering of this age?

Defection from Fellowship

I talk with so many people who are like Demas in their drift away from an intimate relationship with God. I meet them on flights, at parties, and secular gatherings. When they discover I am a clergyman, many of them talk about their growing distance from the church. Then, as the conversation deepens, often I discover that for them, prayer has become infrequent and inconsequential. Often I ask if they are part of any deep fellowship with other believers; most often, they are not.

Demas is a kind of patron for these drifters from the fellowship of the flaming heart. We learn from Paul's words about him that his defection from fellowship with the apostle and his brothers and sisters in Christ in Rome preceded his desertion to go to Thessalonica. If the usual sequence was happening, he broke fellowship and then broke his commitment to loyalty.

Tradition has it that Demas was a native of Thessalonica, and that he was probably converted to Christ when Paul, Silas, Timothy, and Luke were there on Paul's second missionary journey. Like Timothy, he must have left home to serve Christ with Paul. Now, in the midst of the persecution of Christians in Rome, he must have been overcome by the spirit of *deilia*—cowardice and caution. This is the same debilitating spirit that, for a time, threatened to crowd out the Holy Spirit in Timothy. That did not happen because the apostle Paul kept him in touch with the fellowship of the flaming heart.

But what about Demas? I've pictured him on that long, lonely journey from Rome to Thessalonica. Like Jonah, he headed in the wrong direction. Demas left the city of encounter and headed for the city of escape. Surely, being back home brought him temporary sublimation of his smarting, open wound of failure. But in my mind's eye, I see him wandering the streets of that harsh Macedonian city.

I've often wondered if one night he didn't stumble by a small dwelling in which he heard followers of Christ in the Church of Thessalonica singing the early Christian hymn, "Awake, you who sleep, arise from the dead, and Christ will give you light" (Ephesians 5:14). My fond hope for Demas is that he responded to the magnetic pulling power of the Holy Spirit and returned to the fellowship. If so, the red ember in the white ash on the hearth of his heart would have been billowed into flame again. It is not beyond the realm of possibility. It happened to another friend of Paul. I say "friend" with a smile and warmth in my heart. I am talking about John Mark, the author of the first Gospel to be written. His biography could have been titled with the phrase that follows.

The Failure Who Made Good

The story of John Mark is the remarkable account of one who failed, but was rehabilitated by the fellowship of the flaming heart.

It is startling to read Paul's instruction to Timothy about Mark: "Get Mark and bring him with you, for he is useful to me for ministry" (4:11). Useful for ministry? Ten years earlier, Mark had been just the opposite when he deserted Paul at Perga of Pamphylia during the apostle's first missionary journey. Something had happened to change Mark and make him useful in ministry. Let's trace the account of his life.

We first meet Mark during the last week of Jesus' ministry. His mother, Mary, owned the house which was the site of the Upper Room in Jerusalem. Tradition has it that he was part of an underground fellowship which helped stage the triumphal entry of Jesus into the city. I think he was the one who made the arrangements for the Last Supper in his house, and was an observer of the tragic events of Jesus' betrayal, trial, and crucifixion.

In fact, I'm convinced that Mark 14:51 is autobiographical: "A certain young man followed Him [Jesus], having a linen cloth thrown around his naked body. And the young men [soldiers] laid hold of him, and he left the linen cloth and fled from them naked." Apparently, after the Last Supper was concluded in his home, he had retired. Then, later in the evening, he was awakened as Jesus and some of the disciples departed for Gethsemane. He dressed quickly, with only a sheet, and followed after them. From the shadows, he witnessed Jesus in prayer in the garden of Gethsemane. He observed Judas' betrayal and Jesus' arrest. He subsequently lived through the hours of the Lord's trial and Calvary.

It was in the same Upper Room in Mark's home that the disciples met during the excruciating and frightening days of waiting after the crucifixion. His mother, Mary, was one of the first witnesses to the resurrection. As the host of the disciples, Mark must have shared the awesome news that Jesus was resurrected. The disciples continued to meet in that same Upper Room, awaiting the power Jesus had promised. Pentecost happened there, when the Holy Spirit was poured out and the fellowship of the burning heart was begun.

Mark was a participant in the infant church that began to grow in Jerusalem. He became an ardent follower of Christ. Perhaps he was one of those who influenced the conversion of his cousin, Barnabas, who became distinguished for selling his lands and possessions and giving the proceeds to the apostles.

Young Mark came under the influence of Peter, who became his hero, friend, and teacher. From the big fisherman, Mark learned the details of Jesus' life and ministry, and in a personal way, what the Lord could do for a person who trusted Him unreservedly. But Mark also learned how Christ could transform one who had denied Him and had failed. Mark's friendship with Peter was to become one of the most redeeming influences in his life.

Along with Barnabas, Mark became an assistant of Paul on the apostle's first missionary journey. It was at Perga at Pamphylia that Mark deserted. The reason for his defection is not known. Fear, hardship, persecution, must have been part of it. Also, it must have been difficult to measure up to Paul's standards and demanding leadership. And Mark must have missed the warm fellowship of the church in Jerusalem. But most of all, Mark must have realized he did not have what it took to be part of Paul's missionary work.

Up to this time, Mark had been on the receiving end of the inspiration of the church. Now, he was called upon to share his faith. Admitting his inadequacy, he left Paul and Barnabas. We can only imagine the embarrassment Mark felt when he returned to the church in Jerusalem. What excuse could he give? Weakness, lack of courage, cowardice?

Whatever the cause, Paul was adamant that Mark should not go with him and Barnabas on the second missionary journey. Discord arose between the two leaders over Mark's previous defection. Luke records what happened in Acts 15:37-39:

> Barnabas was determined to take with them John called Mark. But Paul insisted that they should not take with them the one who had departed from them in Pamphylia and had not gone with them to the work. Then the contention became so sharp

that they parted from one another. And so Barnabas took Mark and sailed to Cyprus.

———

Think of the pain of being the cause of discord like that. But Barnabas, whose very name means "son of encouragement," was a source of strength to Mark. The fellowship of the flaming heart began the healing process and after Barnabas, another on-fire leader of the church took over.

Mark's hero and friend, Peter, was the one who helped make a strong man in Christ out of a vacillating, frightened defector. In his epistle, Peter calls him "Mark my son" (1 Peter 5:13). Mark became Peter's disciple

> *Nothing could mean more to Mark than the one whom he had failed now saying, "He is useful to me for ministry."*

and interpreter. Peter knew all about failures. He had been one, and Christ had rescued him. As Mark listened to Peter's preaching and shared conversation and companionship, he was able to feel the warmth of the Holy Spirit in Peter's flaming heart. Somewhere along the way, Mark was able to accept forgiveness and make a fresh start.

The result was amazing. The reconciliation for which Christ had died was experienced between Mark and Paul.

The apostle mentions Mark in several of his letters. He commends Mark to the church at Colosse (Colossians 4:10-11), and he shares in Paul's apostolic greeting to Philemon (Philemon 24). And what could be a better affirmation than Paul's request of Timothy to get Mark and bring him with him when he came to Rome? Nothing could mean more to Mark than the one whom he had failed now saying, "He is useful to me for ministry."

Because of the fellowship of the flaming heart, Mark was not only reestablished, but restored. It is very significant that Mark gained firsthand knowledge of Christ's ministry and message from Simon Peter and others in the church at Jerusalem and was the author of the first Gospel to be written.

A Beloved Brother

The warmth of caring concern in the fellowship of the flaming heart in the early church was exemplified in Tychicus. In Acts 20:4, Tychicus is described as an "Asian," one from Asia Minor. Paul's reference to him in his letter to Ephesus calls him "a beloved brother and faithful minister in the Lord…whom I have sent to you…that he may comfort your hearts" (Ephesians 6:21-22).

Four magnificent things distinguish Tychicus: He was a beloved brother, a faithful minister, a comforter—and he was faithful. The bonds of Christ's love, often greater than even the ties of family affection and loyalty, bind us into oneness in the fellowship of the flaming heart. We experience the Holy Spirit flaming in us, galvanizing to one another. Our calling is to serve one another. The words Paul used for Tychicus were "faithful minister." The word "minister" is *diakonos* in Greek, meaning "servant." Our motto in the fellowship is, "How may I serve you?" Christ, who washed the disciples' feet, gives us the challenging example of the humble servants we are called to be to each other. Think of the difference that would make in the contemporary church in America!

And also, Tychicus was a comforter. One of the truly great names for the Holy Spirit is "Comforter." When the Spirit flames in us, we are given supernatural powers to stand by, support, encourage, and inspire one another. But when we think of a comforter, we think of one who helps us in our times of grief. The fellowship of the flaming heart reaches out to help us face the griefs of life. Our life verse for this aspect of the fellowship is,

> Blessed be the God and Father of our Lord Jesus Christ, the Father of mercies and God of all comfort, who comforts us in all our tribulation, that we may be able to comfort those who are in any trouble, with the comfort with which we ourselves are comforted by God (2 Corinthians 1:3-4).

The fourth crowning quality of Tychicus' discipleship dossier was that he was faithful, full of faith in the Lord. Tychicus was loyal, dependable, one on whom the fellowship could count. Before pressing on in this chapter, pause to ask, "Am I a part of a fellowship of people like Tychicus? And would I be distinguished by being a beloved brother, faithful minister, comforter?"

An Informer

Now, a note of reality is sounded by Paul as he alerts Timothy to beware of Alexander the coppersmith. "Alexander the coppersmith did me much harm. May the Lord repay him according to his works. You also must beware of him, for he has greatly resisted our words" (2 Timothy 4:14-15). The verb Paul connects with the word "harm" is *enedeikato*—from the verb *endeiknumi*, meaning "display," "inform," or "do evil to." Alexander was an informer. People who sought to curry favor with the magistrate in Ephesus passed information about the Christians, perhaps even false and slanderous information.

The silver and coppersmiths of Ephesus were not friends of the Christians and the church. So why would Paul have to warn Timothy about Alexander? I suggest that, perhaps, he had been a trusted member of the church, and had become a dangerous defector. One whom Timothy would be inclined to trust, was really an enemy of the cause of Christ.

But note that, coupled with Paul's honest recognition of the danger to the fellowship Alexander could be, the apostle also could trust in the Lord's judgment of his actions.

That's very helpful to us today. We should be able to alert one another to people who have become quislings and antagonists, but we need not take the responsibility of condemnatory judgment unto ourselves. That's up to the Lord! The fellowship of the flaming heart excludes no one, but does honestly recognize the painful fact of those who have excluded themselves, and turned on those who have loved them.

Friends in Need, Indeed!

It is in times of need that the fellowship of the flaming heart provides us with friends, indeed! In Paul's closing greetings, he mentions Prisca and Aquila, who had taken in the apostle while he lived through the turbulent days of ministry in Corinth. They were fellow tentmakers and believers in Christ as Lord. Out of their own difficulties, they knew how to comfort and encourage their friend. They had been driven out of Rome by Claudius, and had come to Corinth. Paul found deep friendship with them during the time in Corinth when he was met with opposition when he attempted to proclaim Christ in Corinth. The Jews reviled him and the rejection impacted Paul's emotions. Before coming to Corinth, he had been driven out of Macedonia and blandly tolerated in Athens. The persistent hostility got to him. Exhausted in body and mind, his spirit had been vulnerable to discouragement. He later had described his condition in his first letter to the church at Corinth: "I was with you in weakness, in fear, and in much trembling" (1 Corinthians 2:3).

However, it was at that low ebb that the apostle received a powerful answer to prayer. The Lord appeared to discouraged Paul and said, "Do not be afraid, but speak, and do not keep silent; for I am with you, and no one will attack you to hurt you; for I have many people in this city" (Acts 18:9-10). Strongest among these friends were Prisca (also called Priscilla) and Aquila.

I think back over 50 years of ministry, and realize that wherever I've been, the Lord's providence and intervention in times of need have been expressed in friends who provided exactly what I needed. I could not have made it without them. They provided fellowship when I felt alone, encouragement when I experienced discouragement, strong support when I took controversial stands, indefatigable prayer partnership when I needed strength, generous giving when projects of ministry were at crossroads, comfort in personal grief, and cheerleading when I was up to bat preaching or teaching. As I write this, a lump forms in my throat and tears of gratitude wet my eyes. Whatever I've been able to accomplish is because of the fellowship of the flaming heart!

Paul went on in extending greetings to people who had been cherished friends. Onesiphorus had come to Paul in prison, and tradition has it that he may have paid for his loyalty with his life. Earlier in this last letter to Timothy, Paul had written, "The Lord grant mercy to the household of Onesiphorus, for he often refreshed me, and was not ashamed of my chain; but when he arrived in Rome, he sought me out very zealously and found me" (2 Timothy 1:16-17). Now Paul greets the household of Onesiphorus. We surmise he was not among them because of his courageous dedication to the apostle.

The Set of the Soul

It is moving to read of the various ways Paul and Timothy's mutual friends had lived out their discipleship because of the set of their souls. Paul mentions Erastus, who had stayed in Corinth. We know little of him except that Paul had once sent him as his emissary into Macedonia (Acts 19:22). And now he probably was a member of the church at Rome.

Trophimus is mentioned also. We remember that it was he whom Paul had brought into the Temple precincts in Jerusalem. He was a Gentile, and the incident was the reason for Paul's first arrest. Obviously, Trophimus had remained faithful, even though the apostle had had to leave him in Miletus sick.

Finally, there are greetings from Eubulus, Pudens, Linus, and Claudia. These are only names to us, but we are sure each one was an invaluable part of the fellowship of the flaming heart. In different ways, they had expressed their love for Christ by extending gracious care to the apostle and to their fellow Christians. Their commitment to Christ was the set of their souls, regardless of the storms of life.

I like the way Ella Wheeler Wilcox puts it:

> *Some ships drive east and some drive west*
> *With the self-same winds that blow*
> *It is the set of the sail and not the gale*
> *That determines where they shall go*
> *And like the winds of the sea*
> *Are the winds of circumstance*
> *In the voyage of life.*
> *It is the set of the soul*
> *That determines the way we shall go.*

CHAPTER TEN

Tending the Eternal Flame— Present in the Present to the Presence

Oscar Levant, the concert pianist, humorist, and some-time movie actor, was giving a concert on the stage of a large auditorium. Suddenly, while he was in the midst of playing an intricate movement of a complicated concerto, the telephone in an offstage office began to ring. The stage manager had forgotten to turn off his ringer.

Levant, who was known for his dry humor expressed in one-liners, kept on playing as if he had not heard the persistent ringing of the phone. Finally, after five minutes—and without missing a note—he turned his head to the audience and said, "If that's for me, tell them I'm busy!" With that, he played on with impeccable concentration. He was present to the present moment.

So often as we live our lives, we are distracted from the present moment by the ringing of a phone, the ping of e-mail alerts, and the whirring sounds of alarm systems. Added to these are the internal, agitating memories of the past and the worrisome disturbances of the future.

I once had a professor who took roll call at the beginning of every class. Each student was required to say, "present" when his name was called. After the professor had read all the names and we all had said "present," he'd look at us and say, "Now lads, are you really present? Are you here for this present moment?"

An important question. There was no way we could learn all the professor wanted to teach us unless he had our full attention.

A man came home one evening, and his wife said, "It's wonderful to have you home!" Then, after observing that he seemed very distracted and not really present to the present, she said, "Yes, it is nice to have you home; now will you please come home?"

Have you ever been at home physically, only to realize that you left your mind in the office, a meeting, or previous conversation? We all have experienced that.

And if you're a parent, have you ever had times when you weren't really listening to your child? Ever had a child ask, "Did you hear what I said?" I remember driving one of my children to school each morning. This was our special time to talk. Often, he would punctuate his paragraphs by asking, "Know what I mean?" It was his way of being sure that my mind had not leapt ahead to the

> *Today is the tomorrow we worried about yesterday. So live today, that it may be a yesterday we won't have to regret.*

day's business and was not concentrating on what he was saying. One morning, he caught me. I realized I had driven for blocks and had not heard a word he said. I had not been present in the present.

We've all had times in conversations when we were not listening. Suddenly, we realize that our minds were elsewhere, or we were so concerned about what we were going to say that we totally missed what a person was trying to communicate.

The reverse is also true. We've all had conversations with people who developed a glassy-eyed, vacant look, and we've wanted to wave our hand in front of their faces and exclaim, "Hey, are you still there!" Or say some inane thing, just to get some reaction. "I just deposited a million dollars in your bank account!" may be a good statement to make when you suspect another person is no longer with you.

You know you are really in trouble if the person doesn't even acknowledge your bogus generosity!

Being present in the present moment is a challenge. When our minds are focused on what has happened in the past or troubled about what may happen in the future, we miss the wonder of now.

Today is the tomorrow we worried about yesterday. So live today, that it may be a yesterday we won't have to regret. Live fully in every moment, as if it were the only moment we'll have.

Present to the Presence in the Present

The secret of living each moment to the fullest is not just being present in the present, but in being present to the Presence in the present. The dual use of "present" is essential. It means that in each present moment, we are to be fully alive, alert, attentive to the presence of Christ.

The apostle Paul teaches us this magnificent truth out of a very painful situation. He describes it in the closing sentences of his final letter to Timothy:

> At my first defense, no one stood with me, but all forsook me. May it not be charged against them. But the Lord stood with me, and strengthened me, so that all the Gentiles might hear. And I was delivered out of the mouth of the lion (4:17).

. . . .

Now, that's being present to the Presence in the present!

Just imagine it. During his second imprisonment in Rome, he was brought before the Forum for a pretrial to establish the charges against him. Alexander, a coppersmith from Ephesus, whom we mentioned in the previous chapter, was probably "state's witness" against him. None of Paul's friends in the church at Rome stood up to defend him. Understandable. It was the Forum, the highest court. All the "grandees" of the Roman Empire were there in all their human power and attire.

Note carefully what possessed Paul's mind in that august moment. He could have been distracted by the fact that he had no one to stand with him. His attention could have been focused on all he had done for his friends, and their lack of courage before the power structure of Rome. Remember that being publicly identified as a Christian would have meant death.

What's crucial for our purposes here is to realize that Paul did not squander his emotions on self-pity or anger at his friends. Also, he could have been in turmoil over the outcome of his trial. Instead, he was present to the presence of Christ in that present moment.

Rather than defending himself, Paul defended Christ. He believed that it was the crowning achievement of his whole ministry to preach Christ before the Roman Forum. The most powerful people in the then-known world had come to watch his trial and to hear the apostle talk about his Savior and Lord.

He lived what he talked about: In life's most difficult times, we have an opportunity to share what Christ means to us.

In the pomp and pageantry of the Forum, Paul's mind was on the presence of Christ. What a magnificent description of the Presence: "The Lord stood with me and strengthened me." The Greek text actually means that the Lord took his stand beside Paul and poured His power into him. Just as the Lord had come to Paul on the Damascus road, and repeatedly, in times of special need, now, in this crisis, at the climax of his ministry, He was there to give him exactly what was required to be faithful and bold.

How did Paul know that Christ was there? Did he actually see Him while others did not? I don't think there was a visible manifestation, for Paul surely would have recorded the reaction of the Roman leaders. Instead, Paul sensed the spiritual presence of the Savior. He expected Him to be there to pour into him intellectual, emotional, and physical strength.

Practicing the Presence

For 30 years, since his conversion, Paul had practiced the Presence. He took Christ at His word: "Lo, I am with you always." The apostle knew that it was not for him to invite Christ into the crises and challenges he faced through the years. The Savior already had been there! He was *always* there. He needed no special invitation. Paul's secret to power was that he acknowledged and acclaimed the Presence all the time.

One of the most important lessons I've learned about prayer and practicing the Presence is that the Lord is always there. My desire to affirm His presence is a result of the impact of His inspiration. Long ago, in both private and public prayer, I stopped asking the Lord to be present, and instead, praised Him for His presence in every situation. Our task is not to convince the Lord to intervene, but to thank Him that He has...and will! Even our prayers for guidance and courage are the result of His instigation to ask for them.

Practicing the Presence is affirming our strong conviction that the Lord always is with us. The affirmation changes everything, beginning with us. We are convinced we are not alone, that the Lord will give us supernatural strength, and that He will use us.

I've discovered that the more I keep focused on practicing the Presence in the present, the more relaxed and free I become. I am able to thank Him for adversities, difficult people, and soul-stretching situations, as well as the blessings He provides. My constant prayer is, "Lord, I know You are here: think, love, and speak through me."

Taking Yourself Before the Lord

Recently, I received a letter from a man called Dick. In the letter, he described the transformation that took place in his life when he discovered the secret of practicing the Presence.

———

"I started my career in the automobile business while still in college in my hometown in Iowa. I was quite successful as a new car dealer for over 35 years. Having that much success and no personal relationship with Christ made me think I was smarter than hell, and could in fact accomplish most anything strictly on my own. I continued a regular attendance in church, but continued to run my own life, and that wasn't very pretty at times.

"I was in control of my own life, and as a result, set a very bad example around me. As I look back, I am embarrassed to have claimed to represent myself as a Christian. I became a community leader as president of the chamber of commerce, chairman of the local economic development group, and nominated by the governor to a high, statewide post.

"I thought I was a pretty big deal. I drank too much and did many other things I am ashamed of today; I always had to be right, and just generally struggled with life. I didn't know anything else. During that period I got a divorce and continued along my downward path. I was very unsettled emotionally, never happy, always looking for something to fill the void that had always existed in my life, always doing more and more business deals trying to fill that void.

"During this time, I became involved in a weekly Bible study group, and I noticed that when I left those morning sessions, I would feel myself be a little 'lighter of step.' I felt good for a moment, but then, as the rigors of the day started, I would be back to running roughshod over life and anyone who got in the way.

"People encouraged me to have a daily devotional, but nothing seemed to work. I tried several daily devotional guides, but I realized that after nearly 50 years of going to church, I didn't know how to pray, and therefore, did none, other than the liturgy on Sunday morning.

"Then, someone gave me a copy of your daily devotional *God's Best for My Life.* On December 29, 1996, I was alone at my home. I woke up early, and was particularly unsettled. Although I was there for Christmas to be with my children, they didn't seem very pleased with me. Business was as usual, bad during that time, and I had too many other business deals going, several of which had problems. And much of my personal life and many of my relationships were a mess.

"The Bible reading that day was a story of King Hezekiah and how he spread out his dilemma before the Lord. I thought about my troubles, and I decided to spread them out before the Lord. As I asked for help, I began to get a flow of ideas that almost overwhelmed me. I knew I would never remember them, so I got up, and got a pencil and paper and started to write these ideas down. At one point during this session, the ideas were flowing so clearly that I actually turned around to see if there was someone in the room with me.

"I was really intrigued with the experience, so I got up early the next day. I read the preface to your book explaining how to pray and practice the Lord's presence. Then, on January 1, I read the scripture you suggested, Jeremiah 29:11-13. I read it over again. It said that God does care about me and wants good things for me. I was on my way to what has become a very close, personal relationship with Christ. I have found I need time with God every day, no matter where I am. *God's Best* and my Bible are my constant companions when I travel."

———

It was wonderful to meet Dick personally when I recently spoke in his hometown. What I have quoted above, he shared with me at a luncheon. Later, he put it into a letter and gave me permission to tell his story. The remarkable thing about Dick is the resiliency his daily devotional time in the Scriptures, reflection, and prayer provides him. I was pleased to learn that he talks to others about the power of the Presence, and gives them devotional guides and Bibles to launch them into the exciting adventure of truly living in the present by being present to the Presence.

No Longer Alone

Dick also shared part of a letter from a friend named Dave who was struggling with life, divorce, alcohol, success, and failure. Dick recognized the symptoms, since he knew them well from his own personal experience. Here's what Dave later wrote about my friend Dick, and the impact of his life on him.

"A close friend and business associate who was aware of the stress that I had been under, called and asked me to come to his house. When I got there, he told me that he wanted to share something with me that has helped him. He had a gift for me. He gave me a copy of a daily devotional, and a copy of a study Bible. He showed me how to use the book, and shared with me what he does every morning when he wakes up. He assured me that if I prayed to God, I would be amazed at the results. Well, first I had to learn how to pray. After eight years in a religious grade school and three years in a parochial high school, I still didn't really know how to pray. This book, *God's Best for My Life,* has become a 'how to' book for me: how to use the Bible, how to pray, how to receive what God wants me to have. I have been at it daily, for over a year, and it is nothing but incredible.

"I have told my friend who gave me the devotional and the Bible that it was the best gift that anyone has ever given me. It is true. He showed me the one thing that I was missing in my life was a personal relationship with God. I never knew what it was that I was missing until I found it.

"Up until that time, I could not get enough of the things that I thought would satisfy my want. I wanted money, I wanted to drink too much and have a good time, and other selfish desires. The more I had, the more I wanted. I could not satisfy the want.

"Now I am happier today than I have ever been in my life; call it pure joy. It is the joy that comes from knowing that God is with us, loves us, forgives us, and wants us to be with Him for eternity. I have less money than I have had, I have not had a drink in over a year, still have problems, my marriage is in deep trouble, my relationship with my dad is sometimes strained, I struggle with personal failures on a daily basis. Life will always be full of difficult challenges. The good news is we don't have to face them alone."

———

Dick's comment about Dave's letter was, "This letter was written four years ago, and David continues to walk with

Christ. He has become a witness for Christ, sharing his own story with others, including his parents, who now also have a daily devotional. He has not had a drink in that time."

"The Lord Is Here!"

The same affirmation of practicing the Presence is the essence of Judy's story. She too ran out of steam running her own life. She needed a fresh billowing of the red ember in the hearth of her heart. Judy is a dynamic business woman. And unlike Dick or Dave, there were no great crises that forced her to confess her need. Instead, there was a growing blandness in her prayers. She confided that she did not feel a close personal relationship with the Lord. No big sins or failures, just a bereft feeling that she had to make it on her own talent, determination, and hard work.

When we talked, I shared with Judy what had happened in my life when I began affirming the Presence of the Lord in every situation and circumstance, rather than furtively thrashing about, trying to bring Him into the present. We both laughed when we thought about the arrogance of thinking we could control the Almighty's movement or actions.

Judy agreed to do an experiment. She made a commitment to begin each day with at least 15 minutes of quiet Scripture reading, meditation, and prayer. Most crucial for the transformation of her life, however, was her further commitment to claim the Lord's presence in the present, and to seek to be fully present to His Presence in each challenge, conversation, or responsibility.

Here's what Judy said about the result of her experiment: "Before beginning the experiment of being present to the Presence, I foolishly thought the Lord would be present only when I could convince Him to pay attention to my needs. Now, prayer is so different: I start the day exclaiming, 'The Lord is here!' I commit my problems and upcoming challenges, reaffirming that the Lord will be there even before I arrive. Every hour, I reassert in my mind, 'The Lord is here.' And you know what? He is!"

> *He…experienced a twofold blessing: Christ stood with him, and Christ strengthened him with the Holy Spirit, reassurance, and resilience.*

Jehovah-Shamma

Judy has learned the secret of praying to the Lord as *Jehovah-Shamma*. This is a great Hebrew name for God. It means, "The Lord is there." This name could well be the motto for those of us who want to make the most of each present moment by practicing the Presence.

It is exciting to be open to what the Lord has planned in each moment. Wonderful things happen. However, if we stop being attentive, aware, and accountable in the present, the "coincidences" stop happening.

Over the years, I have frequently returned to Paternus's advice to his son:

> First of all, my child, think magnificently of God.
> Magnify His providence; adore His power; pray to
> Him frequently and incessantly. Bear Him always
> on your mind; teach your thoughts to reverence
> Him in every place, for there is no place where He is
> not. Therefore, my child, fear and worship, and love
> God; first and last, think magnificently of God.

The places where we live our lives are sacred because the Lord will meet us there. Whether awake or sleeping, at home or at work, with people or alone, speaking or in silence, walking or on your knees, Jehovah-Shamma is there! The more you and I affirm that, the more we will experience Him in the present.

Paul uses a vivid Hebraism to describe how the Lord helped him when he stood before the Roman Forum. "I was delivered out of the mouth of the lion." From Daniel in the lion's den on through Israel's history "the mouth of the lion" was a descriptive term for an enemy of Yahweh and an adversary of His people.

Paul thought magnificently of God in the way he explains how He cared for him. The apostle experienced a twofold blessing: Christ stood with him, and Christ strengthened him with the Holy Spirit, reassurance, and resilience.

We are back to where we began this book. We've talked about the way the omniscient, omnipotent, and omnipresent Christ stands by our side and re-ignites the fire within us with the fire of the Holy Spirit. Christ holds the bellows, and with the Holy Spirit, fuels the red ember in the hearth of our hearts.

Before you close this book, dare to pray this prayer:

> *Lord Christ, like so many, there are times when I feel burned-out inside. Thank you for reassuring me that it is never too late to be set ablaze with passion for life again. I claim that there really is a red ember in the white ash on the hearth of my heart. But I can't billow it to flame by myself. You alone hold the mighty bellows. Pour into me the power of the Holy Spirit. Re-ignite me until I am on fire with convincing intellectual truth, consuming emotional enthusiasm, and a compelling desire to know and do Your will. Here is my mind—think through it; here are my emotions—love through me; here is my will—totally committed to be present to your Presence in the present. Amen.*

Notes

1. From a sermon entitled, "Expect Great Things from God," later published in a collection of sermons: James S. Stewart, *The River of Life* (London: Hodder and Stoughton, 1972), p. 134, emphasis added.

2. © 2004 Sue McCollum. Used by permission.

3. "It's Still the Cross" by Niles Borop, Luke Garrett, Mike Harland, and Kenneth Mullins. © 1995 Niles Borop Music/Centergy Music/Centergetic Music (rights administered by Integrated Copyright Group, Inc.). All rights reserved.

4. Adapted from W.H. Murray, *The Scottish Himalaya Expedition* (1951). Murray is quoting a passage from Goethe's *Faust* (214-30) as freely paraphrased by John Anster, 1835. The research on the origin of this quotation is summarized at www.goethesociety.org/pages/quotescom.html.

5. "What God Hath Promised," from *Annie Johnston Flint Poems,* vol. 1 (Grand Rapids, MI: Zondervan Publishing House, 1944), p. 125.

6. "Great Is Thy Faithfulness" by Thomas O. Chisholm, © 1923. Ren. 1951 Hope Publishing Co. Used by permission.

7. Anonymous.

8. From "In His Hands" by John Campbell Shairp (1819–1885).

9. Excerpted from "The Land of Beginning Again," a poem by Louise Fletcher Tarkington, found in *1000 Quotable Poems,* Thomas Curtis Clark and Esther Gillespie, comp. (New York: Random House, 2000), p. 70.

10. From the poem "God Moves in a Mysterious Way" by William Cowper (1731–1800).

Harvest House Books
by Lloyd John Ogilvie

GOD'S BEST FOR MY LIFE
Better than your fondest hopes and expectations, God wants to give you His best for your life. This classic bestseller offers 365 devotions that invite you to discover, explore, and enjoy your loving Father each day.

PRAYING THROUGH THE TOUGH TIMES
The author gently guides you to pray for God's desires: confidence in His nearness; His grace to love others; and ability to see with His vision, grasping what the future can be when you put it in His hands.

QUIET MOMENTS WITH GOD
These daily prayers will help you nurture a special intimacy with God. You will experience God's blessed assurance as you are comforted by His boundless love and His promises to provide guidance and give strength.

THE RED EMBER IN THE WHITE ASH
Do you sometimes feel tired...burnt out...fearful to engage life? Dr. Ogilvie draws on Scripture to point you to the living and active Holy Spirit. As you see the darkness of fear and discouragement driven out by His flame of godly enthusiasm, you will experience hope and be able to love others with God's love.

IHUMW 248
.4
O34

OGILVIE, LLOYD JOHN
    THE RED EMBER IN THE
    WHITE ASH
CENTRAL LIBRARY
01/07

DISCARD